Butter & SCOTCH

Butter & SCOTCH

RECIPES FROM BROOKLYN'S FAVORITE BAR & BAKERY

ALLISON KAVE & KEAVY LANDRETH

Principal Photography by
Molly Landreth & Jenny Riffle

Additional Photography by Noah Fecks

ABRAMS, NEW YORK

For our
mothers

CONTENTS

The Basics
Cakes, Pies, Toppings & Cocktails

Brunch

Magic Buns 58
Apple-Cheddar Turnovers 68
Allison's Oatmeal 71

BROOKLYN BISCUITS

Brooklyn Biscuits 74
Deli-Style Bacon, Egg & Cheese 76
Biscuits & Gravy 78
BLT 80
Sweet & Savory 81
Smoked Trout Benedict 82
Strawberry Shortcake 85

Yorkshire Popovers 86
Strawberry-Basil Jam 88
Winter Citrus Marmalade 90
Passion Fruit Curd 92
Granola 93
Rhonda's Green Chile Cornbread 94
Mama T's Tuna Quiche 96
Maple-Bacon Cupcakes 99
Manmosa 100
Crown Heights Coffee 101
Pepsi Milk 103
Hair of the Dog Michelada 104

HEIRLOOM BLOODY MARYS

Bloody Mary Gets Fresh 107
Maria Verde 110
Yellow Snapper 111

PICKLED VEGGIES

Pickled Beets & Onions 114
Gibson Onions 115
Spicy String Beans 116
Cumin Carrots 117

Happy Hour

S'mores Bars 120
Kings County Corn Bowl Sundae 125
Negroni Pie 128
Watchamacallthat Pie 131
Twin Peaks Special 134

BOOZY FLOATS

Pretty in Pink 140
ROOT & Beer Float 141
Apple Pie Float 142
Bittersweet 143

HOTTIES

Hot Buttered Scotch 146
Peppermint Patty 147
Porto Quente 148
Rhonda's Ruby Toddy 149
Bitter Medicine 150
Literally & Figuratively 151

Grilled Pineapple 153
Menta Make a Julep 154
Rhubarb Sour 156
Lady Boss Daiquiri 158
Union Street Collins 159

Night

Late Night

In the Beginning...

When I was four, my parents found me hiding in our living room closet, parked between the broom and the vacuum, chugging a bottle of maple syrup.

KEAVY

At five, my mom taught me how to make risotto. She would pull up a stool, hand me a wooden spoon, and I would stir for hours without budging or ever getting bored.

In second grade, my teacher went around the room and asked each of us what we wanted to be when we grew up. I proudly answered that I was planning to work part-time at McDonald's and part-time at Burger King—I couldn't bear to pick just one.

When I was seven, I discovered the joys of "recipe testing." I would raid the kitchen cabinets, pulling out everything that appealed to me: flour, white chocolate (which I would end up eating before it got into the batter), eggs, honey, sugar, fruit, and whatever else was at arm's reach. I would pile everything into a big bowl and mix, not knowing or caring about measurements. Nothing ever turned out quite right, and my mess, as my mother still never tires of reminding me, was never cleaned.

At eight, I discovered my entrepreneurial spirit in the form of a lemonade stand. I would set up the stand every day with my friend Laura. We would hold up signs bigger than our bodies and scream at the few cars that passed down the small side street in front of my house. We would fruitlessly try to sell lemonade, never giving up hope, even when hours would pass without a single sale.

When I entered middle school, I became obsessed with Lynne Rossetto Kasper's cookbook, *The Splendid Table*, and turned every homework assignment into a culinary adventure. When studying the Renaissance, I brought in a giant platter of tagliatelle with caramelized oranges and almonds, and for our lessons on Mexico, I baked off a *pan de muerto* the size of one of the school desks. My essays received Cs, but I discovered that food was a wonderful way to make friends.

In high school, I tried my hand at bartending: mixing vodka with Snapple, doing shots of dark rum and Malibu, or drinking peach schnapps straight from the bottle. This new hobby led me to be grounded for most of my high school years. My mom would look at me and furiously tell me I wasn't allowed out of the house for the next two weeks, and I would look back, smile, and say, "Okay, what are we cooking?"

When I was seventeen, I got my first job as a line cook at a popular restaurant in my hometown, Mount Vernon, Washington. The second day on the job, I chopped the top of my finger off dicing jalapeños. Blood squirted everywhere, and the front-of-house staff screamed as they watched me toss the tip of my finger into the garbage. I wound up getting a bandage on my middle finger that was twice as long as my actual finger, but I didn't care; I had my first war wound, and I couldn't have been happier. I worked doubles on school nights, blasting Ani DiFranco's *Dilate* while scrubbing down low-boys. I smoked pot with the prep cook in the dry goods section of the basement before making veggie burgers, which, if I remember correctly, took me at least ten hours. I befriended the night baker, who would let me help her bake after I had clocked out for the evening, filling me in on all the restaurant gossip.

And after many more glorious and not-so-glorious years in the food industry, at thirty, I found myself having drinks with Allison, discussing our future retail location. We wanted something that was different than your typical bakery: a place that was edgy but built around nostalgia, where our desserts and drinks had integrity, but also a sense of humor. A place that was friendly and inviting but at times could be a little debaucherous. We wanted a place that was just like us.

As soon as I learned of its existence, I begged and begged my mom for an Easy-Bake Oven.

ALLISON

This was back in the eighties, and she was hardly a "helicopter mom," but for some reason, she got it into her head that the tiny 100-watt lightbulb that magically brought little cakes to life would hopelessly disfigure me (or burn our house down). I never got my Easy-Bake Oven (though I have nearly succumbed to impulse-buying one for myself on many a late-night internet browse), but perhaps that unfulfilled desire is what brought me to my present profession.

My mom's concern for my safety might be perceived as bizarrely sporadic: No toy ovens allowed, but whenever I'd get a little cold, she'd whip up some extremely potent hot toddies in lieu of NyQuil. On a visit back to my birthplace in New Mexico, we went on a family hike, and when my parents realized they'd forgotten to pack any water for me and my brother, we all shared a family wineskin. I developed my taste for whiskey and wine from a young age, and it's served me quite well.

We were lucky to travel extensively as a family, and one year we spent the holidays in Champagne, France (you know, where Champagne comes from!). It was there that I experienced my first bite of foie gras, and then my second, and then my fortieth. I couldn't stop eating the stuff and wound up with a stomach of regret late that evening.

Despite this seemingly sophisticated palate, the first time I ever got really drunk (outside of the family home), I was fourteen, majorly crushing on a cute sophomore, and we found ourselves at a homecoming party, with the last pick from the home bar that everyone was raiding. All that we could salvage was a bottle of green crème de menthe. We passed it back and forth, enjoying the minty, slippery liqueur and exchanging swoony, green-toothed smiles. I experienced my first hangover the next day and swore off crème de menthe for many years to come.

Perhaps you're seeing a pattern here? The Robert Heinlein quote under my high school yearbook photo read, "Everything in excess! To enjoy the flavor of life, take big bites." (Yes, I was a nerd who read Heinlein in high school). Indulgence, and overindulgence, were the name of the game for me for many years (name a vice, any vice, and odds are I've sampled it).

Now that I'm all grown up and responsible, I try to temper my indulgences with a bit of moderation, but I'm not always successful. I've made my job about pleasure: both mine and my patrons'. I do not eat simply to survive. I do everything I can to avoid eating something mediocre just because I'm hungry. I want to enjoy every bite that I put in my mouth, and I aim every day to provide that enjoyment for our customers.

Keavy and I decided to open not just a bakery, and not just a bar, but a bar and bakery, because we knew that such a place ought to exist. Why enjoy a massive slice of birthday cake on its own when you can alternate bites with sips of bright, bubbly cava? Why dunk your chocolate chip cookie in a glass of milk when you can dunk it in a White Russian? Butter & Scotch is a place where you can say YES to whatever crazy indulgence you want to experience. You want a vanilla milkshake with a shot of tequila and a slice of Key lime pie swirled in? Yes, we will happily make that for you (and great idea, by the way).

After all the time we've spent thinking about, talking about, and building this place, it's incredibly rewarding to look over at Keavy, my partner on this tumultuous ride, and be able to say, *We did it*. We created something that perfectly reflects our personalities, our passions, and our histories, and we did it as a team. I can't wait to see where our next crazy ambition takes us!

How We See It

OUR BAKING & BOOZING PHILOSOPHY

It all started over a couple of pitchers of sangria. We had both grown our businesses as far as they could go: Keavy owned Kumquat Cupcakery, and Allison owned First Prize Pies, both based in Brooklyn. Both were dessert businesses with very similar models: weekend markets, a bit of wholesale, and some catering, without brick-and-mortar locations. We were tired! Tired of being sherpas, shlepping tents and bags of pies and cupcakes all over town to our various markets, wholesale outlets, and catering gigs. We were ready to create a place to call home, and we didn't want it to be *just* another bakery.

After draining a few glasses, we figured it out. We both love to dine out in NYC, we both love well-made drinks, and we both love great desserts. But we realized there wasn't anywhere in town where one could go after dinner to enjoy a really well-made dessert and a craft cocktail. We wanted to create a space for fun, where adults could go to feel like kids and really indulge, without being forced into a fancy plated pairing.

Butter & Scotch is all about the FUN. This isn't where you go to get freeze-dried carrot foam plated with tweezers (though that stuff can be pretty cool, too). We care a lot about using great ingredients, making things from scratch, and doing things the right way—but we do this for an end result that's indulgent, rustic, and sometimes really goofy!

Our menu runs the gamut from untouchable classics like Cherry Pie (page 137) to more out-there creations like Jell-Ohh Shots (page 221) and Boozy Shakes (page 210). And we don't shy away from bringing in "lowbrow" ingredients when appropriate: We serve our Pimento Cheese (page 202) with Triscuits, because they are a perfect cracker and the ideal vehicle for that salty, spicy, cheesy concoction. Basically, if our customers are smiling and happily indulging whatever cravings they're experiencing, we're doing our job.

The Basics

Cakes, Pies, Toppings & Cocktails

In this chapter, we'll cover the **core recipes** that we adapt for a lot of our desserts and drinks—the **building blocks** that you can use to create a wide variety of delicious **baked goods** and **cocktails**.

Cake Stuff

Keavy's a cake person. She loves them all: flourless, boxed (Funfetti! hello!), straight vanilla, carrot cake piled with junk—heck, she even gets excited over fruitcake. She loves cake straight from the oven without any frosting or even straight from the fridge eaten with her hands. The only kind of cake she *doesn't* like is a dry cake. Below are a few helpful tips to keep your cake nice and moist.

MIXER SPEED

The general rule of thumb when making a cake is to start with the mixer on high and end with it on low. The more the butter and sugar beat together during the creaming process, the fluffier your cake will be once it comes out of the oven. However, once the flour is added to your batter, this rule no longer applies. As with all gluten-full baked goods, the less the dough is worked once the flour goes into the bowl, the more tender and moist the end product will be. This is because of the almighty glutens in the flour that tense up when worked too much. Once you get to this stage, you should never turn the mixer above its lowest speed.

SUGAR & FAT

Sugar and fat play an incredibly important role in most baked goods: They provide flavor and keep the cake tender. Fat comes from a few different sources when making cakes: eggs, butter, and milk are the most common, but you can also use oil, sour cream, or even shortening (though this offers up the least flavor). Sugar crystals work with these fats to coat the flour and decrease the development of tough glutens.

AIR

Air in cake batter is very important to creating a fluffy, moist cake. When you cream together your butter and sugar, it creates bubbles that will help your cake stay tender during the baking process. As in the case of our Birthday Cake (page 167), you can also get this from beating and folding egg whites into your batter.

However, once the cake is baked, air turns into the cake's worst enemy. It's air that will make a beautiful fluffy cake turn stale. One way to prevent this from happening is to wrap the cake rounds in plastic if they are not being frosted immediately. Once they are frosted, the icing seals the cake and acts as its own wrap. After a frosted cake is cut into, either put it in a cake dome or large Tupperware, or lay a few pieces of plastic wrap over the area where the cake was cut.

TEMPERATURE

For cakes, the "danger zone" is between 33 and 50°F (0.5 to 10°C), which tends to cover the temperature of most refrigerators. This range of settings helps to accelerate the drying-out process of cakes. Luckily for us, cakes are perfectly fine at room temperature for up to a week—we even think they get better after a day of rest.

You can also freeze your cakes. If you want to bake your cake but don't need to serve it for a few days, you can wrap it up well in plastic or put it in a Ziploc bag and stick it in the freezer, and it will be as good as new once it's brought back to room temperature. This can be done to unfrosted cake rounds or even the whole cake once it's frosted. Freezing also works for regular and mini-size cupcakes. To quote Keavy's mother, "I've never met a cake that didn't freeze."

CUPCAKE BATTERS

Before we came together to create Butter & Scotch, Keavy owned a mini-cupcake company called Kumquat Cupcakery. It was born in 2008 in her three-hundred-square-foot apartment in Williamsburg, Brooklyn. She had become obsessed with trying to create the perfect cupcake and was making hundreds of them a week for friends. The transition from regular-size cupcakes to mini-cupcakes was a purely logistical one—she simply didn't have enough room in her apartment to house all the cupcakes that she was making on a daily basis.

Salted Caramel Chocolate Cupcakes (page 23)

Lemon Lavender Cupcakes (page 21)

Vanilla Cupcakes

When Keavy made the switch to minis, she realized that the cupcake batter needed to change dramatically to prevent these little bites from drying out too quickly, and because they were so little, she needed a batter that was going to pack a punch. While browsing the internet for inspiration, she came across a brownie recipe, and thought, *What if I took out the chocolate and upped the amount of flour?* It worked perfectly! The large amount of melted butter took out some of those air bubbles that are good in larger cupcakes, but were drying out her mini cupcakes, and it resulted in a very flavorful but extremely dense and moist cake that wouldn't dry out too fast.

These base recipes can be easily manipulated to create a large range of mini-cupcake flavors. They can also be used to make larger cupcakes and cakes; however, because of their nature, they result in much more of a pound cake texture and not a classically fluffy cupcake. We advise adding fresh fruit or fruit purees to the batter if scaling up, to ensure that you get a moist cake.

Preheat the oven to 350°F (175°C). Line cupcake pans with paper liners.

In a large bowl, combine the flour, baking powder, and salt and set aside. In the bowl of a stand mixer fitted with the whisk attachment, add the sugar and pour the melted butter over the top. Mix on medium speed for about 1 minute to cool the butter. Add the eggs and vanilla to the butter mixture all at once and mix until fully

1½ cups (190 g) unbleached all-purpose flour

1 teaspoon baking powder

½ teaspoon kosher salt

¾ cup (150 g) sugar

1 cup (2 sticks / 225 g) unsalted butter, melted

4 large eggs

2 teaspoons vanilla extract

Makes 4 dozen mini-cupcakes or 1 dozen regular-size cupcakes

incorporated. Turn the mixer down to the lowest speed and add the flour mixture. Mix on low until the batter becomes smooth. Do not turn the mixer to high speed, or else it will overwork the flour and will create a drier cupcake.

Spoon the batter into the prepared pans. Bake minis for 8 to 10 minutes, until the cupcakes have puffed up and are set. Bake regular-size cupcakes for 12 to 14 minutes. Wait until they're completely cool to frost.

Variations

Lemon Lavender Cupcakes
Add the zest of 1 lemon after mixing in the flour mixture. Top with Lavender Frosting (page 29).

Peanut Butter Banana Honey Cupcakes
Fold in 1 ripe, mushed-up banana after incorporating the flour. Top with Peanut Butter Frosting (page 29) and a drizzle of honey.

Strawberry Cupcakes
Add 1 cup (165 g) finely chopped fresh or frozen strawberries after mixing in the flour. Top each cupcake with Keavy's Favorite Vanilla Frosting (page 26) and a slice of fresh strawberry.

Coffee Caramel Bourbon Cupcakes
Add 2 tablespoons instant coffee powder to the melted butter before pouring it over the sugar. Top with Keavy's Favorite Vanilla Frosting (page 28) and Caramel Bourbon Sauce (page 41).

Chocolate Cupcakes

Like the Vanilla Cupcakes (page 20), this is simply a brownie recipe with added baking powder. It's incredibly rich and dense and packed full of unsweetened cocoa, making it less sweet than your average chocolate cupcake. As with brownies, we prefer these slightly underbaked, so they'll be even more gooey and decadent.

This recipe can be played around with to create a range of different chocolate cupcake combinations. At right are our three favorite variations.

¾ cup (95 g) unbleached all-purpose flour

½ cup (50 g) unsweetened cocoa powder

2 teaspoons baking powder

2 teaspoons kosher salt

¾ cup (150 g) sugar

1 cup (2 sticks / 225 g) unsalted butter, melted

4 large eggs

2 teaspoons vanilla extract

Preheat the oven to 350°F (175°C). Line cupcake pans with paper liners.

In a large bowl, combine the flour, cocoa powder, baking powder, and salt and set aside. In the bowl of a stand mixer fitted with the whisk attachment, add the sugar and pour the melted butter over the top. Mix on medium speed for about 1 minute to cool the butter. Add the eggs and vanilla to the butter mixture all at once and mix until fully incorporated. Turn the mixer down to the lowest speed and add the flour mixture. Mix on low until the batter becomes smooth. Do not turn the mixer to high speed, or else it will overwork the flour and will create a drier cupcake.

Spoon the batter into the prepared pans. Bake minis for 8 to 10 minutes, until the cupcakes have puffed up and are set. Bake regular-size cupcakes for 12 to 14 minutes. Wait until they are completely cool to frost.

**Makes 4 dozen mini-cupcakes or
1 dozen regular-size cupcakes**

Variations

Salted Chocolate Caramel Cupcakes

Top each cupcake with Dark Chocolate Frosting (page 27),
Classic Caramel Sauce (page 40), and a pinch of kosher or
Maldon salt.

Chocolate Raspberry Cupcakes

Top each cupcake with Keavy's Favorite Vanilla Frosting (page
28) and a fresh raspberry.

Chocolate Peanut Butter Cupcakes

Once the chocolate cupcakes have cooled, use the wider end
of a chopstick to poke a hole into the center of each. Using a
piping bag with a round tip, pipe peanut butter into each hole.
Top with Peanut Butter Frosting (page 29).

FROSTING

Remember the frosting you used to find in your refrigerator as a kid? In that pint-size container with the flimsy plastic lid? We wanted something that would taste just like that . . . but better.

We played around with many variations of buttercreams, but they were often either too sweet or would leave a lingering butter flavor in our mouths. We experimented with cream cheese frostings, but didn't like the way the cream cheese flavor would overpower the flavor of the cake. It was when we decided to create the frosting with equal parts butter and cream cheese that all the flavors came together perfectly. The butter and cream cheese balanced each other out so that neither one overpowered the other, while also letting the flavors in our cakes shine.

This frosting is so incredibly easy to make and very versatile; however, when adding different ingredients to it, make sure to steer clear of anything too acidic like juices or fruit purees. They will break down the sugars and make the frosting too soft. We've found that the best way to get fruit flavor into your cakes and cupcakes is to add it into the batter or place the fresh fruit right on top of the frosting.

Dark Chocolate Frosting

In the bowl of a stand mixer fitted with the paddle attachment, cream the butter, making sure to stop the mixer every so often to scrape down the sides and bottom of the bowl. It's important to have all the butter nice and soft so you don't get any clumps of cold butter when trying to pipe the frosting (see Pro Tip). Next, add the cream cheese a quarter at a time on medium speed. When it is incorporated, add the melted chocolate chips. Turn the mixer to the lowest speed and slowly add the sugar and cocoa powder. Once they are mixed into the butter and cream cheese mixture, crank the mixer up to high speed and beat it for 30 seconds, until fully blended and fluffy.

PRO TIP: If the butter is a little too cold when starting this recipe, use a kitchen torch to warm the bottom of the bowl as it's mixing and the butter will pull away from the sides on its own. Just be sure not to torch it too much or the butter will melt completely.

2 cups (4 sticks / 455 g) unsalted butter, at room temperature

1 pound (455 g) cream cheese, at room temperature

1 cup (175 g) semisweet chocolate chips, melted

2 pounds (910 g) confectioners' sugar

1 cup (95 g) unsweetened cocoa powder

**Makes enough for one 8-inch (20-cm) cake,
4 dozen mini-cupcakes,
or 1 dozen regular-size cupcakes**

Keavy's Favorite Vanilla Frosting

In the bowl of a stand mixer fitted with the paddle attachment, cream the butter, making sure to stop the mixer every so often to scrape down the sides and bottom of the bowl. It's important to have all the butter nice and soft so you don't get any clumps of cold butter when trying to pipe the frosting (see Pro Tip, page 27). Next, add the cream cheese a quarter at a time on medium speed. When it is incorporated, add the vanilla. Turn the mixer to the lowest speed and slowly add the sugar. Finally, crank the mixer up to high speed and beat it for 30 seconds, until fully blended and fluffy.

Makes enough for one 8-inch (20-cm) cake, 4 dozen mini-cupcakes, or 1 dozen regular-size cupcakes

2 cups (4 sticks / 455 g) unsalted butter, at room temperature

1 pound (455 g) cream cheese, at room temperature

2 tablespoons vanilla extract

2 pounds (910 g) confectioners' sugar

Variations

Lavender Frosting

When making lavender frosting, we like using
dried lavender buds that we grind up with a spice grinder.
You don't want to use these whole or put in too much—
they are very potent and can taste like you are eating soap.

Add 1 teaspoon ground lavender
buds right after adding the confectioners' sugar.

(You can find dried lavender buds for cooking at some holistic grocery stores as well as
some flower shops. But when in doubt, you can easily find them online.)

Peanut Butter Frosting

This frosting tastes like the inside of Reese's Pieces and is
highly addictive, so you may want to double the recipe in
preparation for a lot of nibbling!

Add ½ cup (120 ml) smooth or chunky peanut butter
and 1 teaspoon kosher salt right after adding
the confectioners' sugar.

PIE CRUST

A lot of the tips here were learned through many years (more than twenty years, in fact!) of baking pies, first as a hobbyist, and then professionally through Allison's previous business, First Prize Pies. She founded that as a little side business in 2010 after winning a pie contest, and it quickly became a full-time career. Allison loves all kinds of baking and cocktail-crafting, but pie is and always will be her core passion. Nothing is as soothing and inspiring as rolling out a round of dough and building a beautiful pie.

Crust: It's a pie-baker's calling card, the paramount element of any pie. Many bakers, both hobbyists and pros, are intimidated by pie crust, but there are a few key tips that will help you achieve flaky, buttery, tender crust every time.

DON'T OVERWORK THE DOUGH

- Are you accustomed to making pasta? Maybe you're a bread baker? Take everything you know about handling those types of dough and do the opposite! When making pie dough, the ingredients should never be completely blended. Rather, you should be able to see all the discrete components even when you're done (lumps of butter, wisps of flour). Handle it only until it just holds together, then leave it alone to chill out for a bit. (We all need some time to ourselves!)

KEEP IT COLD

- Cold is the enemy of gluten, and gluten is the enemy of tender, flaky crusts (though you need a bit of it for everything to hold together). To avoid gluten development, keep all your ingredients cold (you can even put flour in the freezer for a while before you're ready to make dough).

FATTY FAT FAT FAT

- Use a lot of fat. Don't like fat? We don't believe you. Can't eat fat? On a diet? Don't eat pie right now. The more fat you've got in your crust, the better it will taste and the better its texture. We use European-style cultured butter with a butterfat content of at least 83 percent. We also use whole milk instead of water—another way to inject more fat into the crust, and a key ingredient for getting it super flaky.

SEASON IT UP!

- Crust is the savory foil to the sweet fillings we put inside it, and it should be well seasoned, with a flavor all its own. Ours tastes so good on its own, we like to sprinkle leftover scraps of pie dough with cinnamon-sugar, bake 'em up, and give them out as off-menu treats. (We call them "Pie Cookies"!)

Here are the recipes for our core pie crusts: a perfect, classic butter crust for fruit and custard pies, and a graham cracker crust to put all other graham cracker crusts to shame!

Roll the Dough

INSTRUCTIONS

1. Let the dough rest at room temperature for 5 to 10 minutes, then sprinkle
with flour. \ 2. Starting from the center and using even pressure,
roll the dough, rotating it between each pass of the rolling pin. \ 3. Be sure to lift
the dough off the counter periodically to prevent sticking, and add more flour as
needed. \ 4. Gently lift the dough into your pie pan.

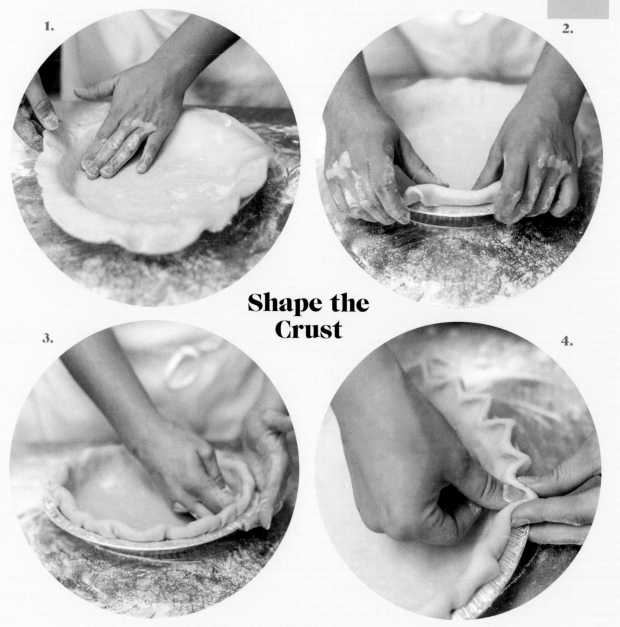

1.

2.

3.

4.

Shape the Crust

INSTRUCTIONS

1. Carefully press the dough into the bottom of the pie pan.
2. Fold the overhang under to form a thick, rolled edge. \ 3. Press the dough along the inner sides of the pie pan. \ 4. Using a gentle pinching motion, crimp the rolled edge of the dough all the way around (you can also use the tines of a fork for an easy decorative option).

All-Butter Pie Crust

Cut the butter into ½-inch (12-mm) cubes. In a liquid measuring cup, stir together the milk and vinegar. On a large clean cutting board or in a large shallow bowl, toss the flour, sugar, and salt together lightly to blend. Add the butter and cut it into the flour using a pastry blender. Work quickly and gently, using a straight up-and-down motion. Avoid using your fingers, which will warm the butter.

Once the butter is roughly the size of small peas or lentils, spread the mixture out to expose as much surface area as possible. Drizzle about half of the milk mixture over the flour, then toss the mixture together using a large spoon or bench scraper. Repeat the process with the rest of the liquid.

You should now have a dough that will just hold together when pressed against the side of the bowl, with visible bits of butter. If you need to add more liquid to bind, do so with more cold milk, adding 1 tablespoon at a time.

Cover the dough tightly with plastic wrap and refrigerate it for at least 1 hour before using, to let the gluten relax. The dough can be stored in the fridge for up to 1 week, well wrapped, or in the freezer for up to 2 months.

Makes enough for one double-crust 10-inch (25-cm) pie

i cup (8 ounces / 225 g) cold unsalted European-style cultured butter

½ cup (120 ml) cold whole milk, plus more if needed

1 tablespoon apple cider vinegar

12 ounces (340 g / approximately 2¾ cups) unbleached all-purpose flour

2 tablespoons sugar

1 tablespoon kosher salt

Graham Cracker Crust

We make our own graham crackers at the shop, exclusively for use in our pie crusts. This may seem excessive in this age of instant gratification, but we challenge you to take the time to whip up a from-scratch graham cracker crust, and give it the Pepsi Challenge against the store-bought kind. You'll find it very difficult to ever go back to the quick-'n'-easy way!

6 Graham Crackers (opposite) or 6 store-bought graham crackers

5 to 8 tablespoons (70 to 115 g) unsalted butter, melted

Crumble the graham crackers into the work bowl of a food processor and process until they're finely ground. You should have about 1½ cups (175 g). Pour the butter into the crumbs and process until the mixture has the texture of wet sand. Firmly press the crumbs against the sides of a 10-inch (25-cm) pie pan, then against the bottom of the pan. Refrigerate the crust for at least 15 minutes. The crust can be refrigerated for up to 1 week, or frozen, wrapped in plastic, for up to 2 months.

OPTIONAL: We don't find it necessary to bake our graham crusts before filling them, but if you want to ensure a totally dry crust, bake it at 350°F (175°C) for about 10 minutes, and allow it to cool completely before filling.

Makes enough for one single-crust 10-inch (25-cm) pie

GRAHAM CRACKERS

Makes 12 to 15 large graham crackers

While many recipes for graham crackers call for "graham" or whole-wheat flour, we've found that all-purpose flour works just as well. If you want to experiment, you can replace half of the all-purpose flour in this recipe with whole-wheat flour for a nuttier flavor and more crumbly texture.

In a large bowl or stand mixer fitted with the paddle attachment, cream together the brown sugar and butter until light and fluffy. Beat in the honey, milk, and vanilla until blended. In a medium bowl, whisk together the flour, baking soda, cinnamon, and salt until combined. Add the dry ingredients to the wet ingredients and beat until just combined. Turn the dough out onto a sheet of plastic, wrap it tightly, and refrigerate for about 2 hours or overnight.

Preheat the oven to 350°F (175°C). Divide the dough in half. On a well-floured surface, roll half the dough into a long rectangle about ⅛ inch (3 mm) thick. The dough will be sticky; flour as needed. Cut the dough into 6 to 8 even rectangles. Transfer them to a parchment-lined baking sheet, and repeat with the rest of the dough.

Bake for 25 minutes, until the crackers are golden brown and slightly firm around the edges, rotating the sheets halfway through. Allow them to cool on the sheets. The crackers can be stored in an airtight container for up to 1 week.

½ cup (110 g) firmly packed dark brown sugar

¼ cup (½ stick / 55 g) unsalted butter, at room temperature

3 tablespoons clover honey

3 tablespoons whole milk

1 tablespoon vanilla extract

6 ounces (175 g / approximately 1¼ cups) unbleached all-purpose flour, plus extra for rolling

½ teaspoon baking soda

¼ teaspoon ground cinnamon

½ teaspoon kosher salt

ICE CREAM TOPPINGS

When it comes to toppings on ice cream, we differ slightly: Allison likes to pile on the STUFF: gummy bears, sprinkles, nuts, cherries, cake, cookie bits . . . the list goes on! Keavy likes to keep it simple: just vanilla ice cream and either caramel sauce or hot fudge. At the shop, we serve our hot fudge sundae the classic way, with hot fudge, whipped cream, and a cherry, but if you happen to swing by, try ordering your sundae "Allison style" and see what happens.

Hot Fudge

Hot fudge is what would happen if caramel sauce and chocolate sauce had a baby, and it's one of the most delicious things on this planet. When training someone new at the shop, we can't stress to them enough the importance of using an excessive amount of hot fudge on ice cream sundaes. Every spoonful of a hot fudge sundae, brownie sundae, or even banana split, should have at least a little bit of hot fudge attached to it.

Hot fudge doesn't only have to be used on ice cream, either. We use it for many of our hot drinks: hot chocolate, mochas, and our Peppermint Patty (page 147).

⅔ cup (165 ml) heavy cream

½ cup (120 ml) light corn syrup (see Note)

⅓ cup (75 g) firmly packed dark brown sugar

¼ cup (25 g) unsweetened cocoa powder

¼ teaspoon kosher salt

6 ounces (170 g) bittersweet chocolate, chopped

2 tablespoons unsalted butter

1 teaspoon vanilla extract

In a medium saucepan, combine the cream, corn syrup, brown sugar, cocoa powder, salt, and half of the chocolate. Bring the mixture to a boil and remove from the heat. Whisk in the remaining chocolate, the butter, and vanilla immediately. Use the hot fudge right away or store it in the refrigerator in an airtight container for up to 1 month. Reheat it in a microwave or on the stovetop when ready to use.

NOTE: We know that nowadays, a lot of folks try to avoid products with corn syrup in them. One thing to keep in mind is the very big difference between regular corn syrup and the high-fructose corn syrup you find in super-sweet sodas (and even loaves of sandwich bread!). While both contain a lot of sugar, the latter has highly concentrated amounts that really aren't good for one's health.

While we don't use corn syrup in most of our desserts, there are a few occasions where you need to use an invert sugar (a sugar that maintains a syrup state) without adding an unwanted flavor. If you're completely opposed to using corn syrup, you can substitute honey here, but be aware that you'll definitely get a pronounced honey flavor (which, depending on your palate, might be a great thing!).

Makes 3 cups (720 ml); enough for about 6 sundaes

Classic
Caramel Sauce

This is our go-to caramel sauce. It takes about five minutes to make and is absolutely delicious on ice cream, cake, pies, or even just a spoon. This sauce should come down to warm or room temperature before you use it, which typically takes about thirty minutes, but if you are like us—terribly impatient—you can cool it down in about half the time by pouring the hot caramel sauce onto a baking sheet and popping it into the refrigerator.

Like most of the recipes in this section, it's super easy to tweak! At right are a few variations we use at the shop.

1 cup (200 g) sugar

3 tablespoons unsalted butter

¾ cup (180 ml) heavy cream

¼ teaspoon kosher salt

In a small saucepan, combine the sugar, butter, and ¼ cup (60 ml) water. Make sure the sugar is completely wet; if it's not, add a tablespoon or two more water. Over medium heat, bring the mixture to a boil. As the sugar boils, the water will evaporate and the sugar and butter will begin to caramelize. When the sugar turns a dark honey shade, remove from the heat, add the cream and salt immediately, and whisk everything together—be careful, as the mixture will release a lot of hot steam! Pour the caramel into a heatproof dish and let it cool before using, at least 30 minutes. Store in an airtight container in the refrigerator for up to 1 month.

**Makes 2 cups (480 ml);
enough for about 4 sundaes**

Variations

Caramel Bourbon Sauce

Add ¼ cup (60 ml) bourbon (it doesn't have to be top-shelf, but use something you'd be happy to drink!) after the heavy cream.

Spicy Ginger Caramel Sauce

Add 1 teaspoon ground dried ginger, 1 tablespoon grated peeled fresh ginger, and ½ teaspoon cayenne after the heavy cream.

Salted Chocolate Caramel Sauce

When the classic caramel sauce has been removed from the heat and placed in a heatproof bowl, add ½ cup (50 g) unsweetened cocoa powder and ¾ teaspoon more kosher salt. The cocoa powder will suck up some of the liquid, which makes for a much thicker sauce than the classic caramel sauce. If you want the sauce to be a bit thinner, you can add ¼ cup (60 ml) more heavy cream to the original recipe, either before or after adding the cocoa, before it cools completely.

Marshmallow Sauce

There's a well-kept secret in the baking world: Marshmallows, although seemingly conjured by magicians and scientists, are actually really easy to make! Have your friends over for an ice cream party, bust out some homemade marshmallow sauce, and they will think you are the most talented baker of all time.

¼ cup plus 2 tablespoons (90 ml) cold water

1 teaspoon unflavored powdered gelatin

¾ cup (150 g) sugar

¼ cup (60 ml) light corn syrup (see Note, page 39)

½ teaspoon vanilla extract

In the bowl of a stand mixer fitted with the whisk attachment, add ¼ cup (60 ml) of the cold water and the gelatin. Set it aside so the gelatin can bloom ("blooming" gelatin is the industry term for allowing it to hydrate and soften). In a small saucepan, combine the sugar, corn syrup, and remaining 2 tablespoons water. Mix the ingredients together so that none of the sugar is dry. Put the saucepan over medium heat and attach a candy thermometer to the inside of the pan so that it's touching the sugar. Bring the mixture to a boil. Once the sugar mixture gets up to 250°F (120°C), remove it from the heat. Turn the mixer on low speed and carefully pour the hot sugar mixture into the gelatin mixture. Be careful to avoid pouring the hot sugar mixture toward the whisk; aim instead for the space between the whisk and the side of the bowl. This will prevent dangerous hot sugar splashes! Once you've added all of the liquid, gradually turn the mixer up to high speed and whisk it until the mixture has at least doubled in volume and is bright white. Mix in the vanilla and turn off the mixer.

Use immediately. If not using right away, store the sauce in an airtight container at room temperature and warm it in the microwave or on the stovetop when you need it. The marshmallow sauce will keep for up to 1 month at room temperature.

Makes 2 cups (480 ml); enough for 4 to 6 sundaes

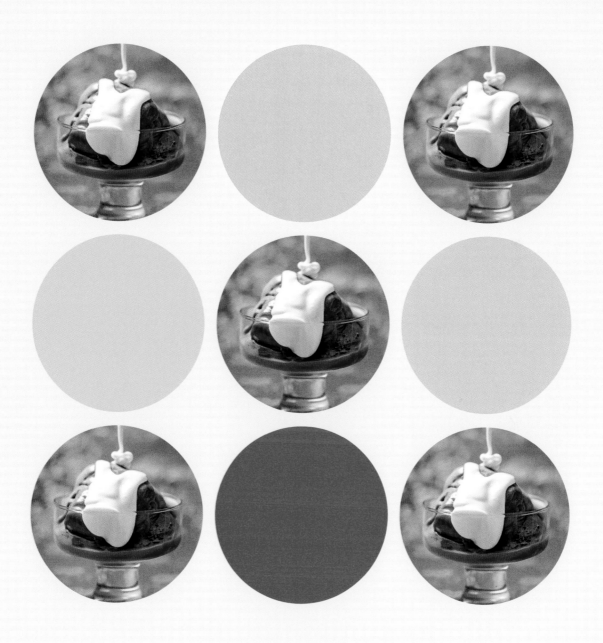

Crushed Toffee

Sprinkling crushed toffee onto your sundae, cake, pudding (or any dessert really!) is a great way to add a little seasoning (it has a good amount of salt) and a great textural component.

½ cup (1 stick / 115 g) unsalted butter

½ cup (100 g) sugar

½ teaspoon kosher salt

Line a baking sheet with a silicone mat or butter it liberally, making sure to get the corners.

In a saucepan, combine the butter, sugar, and salt with 1 tablespoon water and bring them to a boil over medium-high heat. Cook for 5 to 10 minutes, until a candy thermometer reads 300°F (150°C) and the sugar begins to brown. Immediately remove the pan from the heat and pour the hot toffee onto the baking sheet. Allow it to cool completely, then shatter the toffee with a mallet (very cathartic!) or in a food processor.

Makes 1 cup (160 g) crushed toffee bits; enough for 4 sundaes

Whipped Cream

Whipped cream is the queen of all dessert toppings. It goes on nearly everything we serve at the shop. On a busy night, we may need to make at least 6 quarts (5.7 L) in order not to run out in the middle of service.

In the bowl of a stand mixer fitted with the whisk attachment, combine the cream, sugar, and vanilla. Mix on high speed until the cream forms soft peaks. Serve immediately, or refrigerate in an airtight container for up to 24 hours (you may need to whisk the cream again to fluff a bit more air into it after it sits in the refrigerator).

2 cups (480 ml) heavy cream

2 tablespoons sugar

1½ teaspoons vanilla extract

Makes 3 cups (720 ml); enough for 6 sundaes

Candied Pecans

Warning! These pecans are highly addictive. They are well seasoned with salt, incredibly buttery, and crunchy from the caramelized sugar. We could eat these by the handful . . . and often do.

Preheat the oven to 350°F (175°C).

In a medium bowl, toss together the pecans, butter, oil, brown sugar, and salt until the pecans are totally coated. Spread them onto a baking sheet and roast, tossing every 5 minutes, until the pecans are fragrant and the sugar has caramelized, 20 to 30 minutes. Store them in an airtight container at room temperature for up to 2 weeks.

2 cups (240 g) pecans, chopped into small pieces

¼ cup (½ stick / 55 g) unsalted butter, melted

1 tablespoon canola oil

¼ cup (55 g) firmly packed dark brown sugar

1¼ teaspoons kosher salt

Makes 2 cups (240 g)

BEHIND THE BAR

Creating cocktails is not unlike baking: Both require precision, practice, and creativity. At Butter & Scotch, we take a playful approach to all things and love to experiment with syrups, infusions, and techniques to create cocktails that mirror the fun, indulgent vibe of our bakery and bar.

Cocktail Syrups

While they may intimidate home bartenders, the sweet syrups that are a key ingredient to most craft cocktails are called "simple" syrups for a reason. Made with simple ratios, and endlessly adaptable with various infusions, homemade syrups are a great way to add a little something extra to your cocktails. Here are a few of our favorites.

SIMPLEST SIMPLE SYRUP

Makes 2 cups (480 ml)

This is the backbone syrup, an essential component of any bar. The recipe is impossible to forget: equal parts sugar and water—that's it! This is also a great way to sweeten nonboozy beverages like iced coffee, iced tea, and lemonade without having to stir for ages to dissolve granulated sugar in a cold beverage.

1 cup (200 g) sugar (play around with white, brown, and raw sugar to get different flavors)

In a small saucepan, heat the sugar and 1 cup (240 ml) water over medium heat, until the sugar has completely dissolved. Store the syrup in an airtight container in the fridge for up to 1 month.

RICH SIMPLE SYRUP

Makes 2 cups (480 ml)

Slightly thicker, richer, and sweeter than 1:1 simple syrup, this one is great in a classic old fashioned.

2 cups (400 g) sugar (play around with white, brown, and raw sugar to get different flavors)

In a small saucepan, heat the sugar and 1 cup (240 ml) water over medium heat, until the sugar has completely dissolved. Store the syrup in an airtight container in the fridge for up to 1 month.

HONEY / HOT HONEY SIMPLE SYRUP

Makes 2 cups (480 ml)

Honey lends a special, fragrant type of sweetness to both cocktails and desserts. We love using it in classic cocktails like daiquiris, and it's an integral part of the traditional hot toddy. We also make a spicy version of this syrup for our Honeychile Rider cocktail (page 186), using chile-infused Mike's Hot Honey (one of our favorite ingredients ever, delicious on everything from pizza to ice cream!).

1 cup (240 ml) honey (varying types of honey yield different flavors; play around to find one you love!) or Mike's Hot Honey

In a small saucepan, heat the honey and 1 cup (240 ml) water over medium heat until the honey has dissolved. Store the syrup in an airtight container in the fridge for up to 2 months.

MOLASSES SIMPLE SYRUP

Makes 2 cups (480 ml)

A key component of our Menta Make a Julep cocktail (page 154), this syrup has a beautiful dark brown hue and lends a slightly bitter cane sugar flavor to any drink.

1 cup (240 ml) light molasses (blackstrap is a bit overpowering)

In a small saucepan, heat the molasses and 1 cup (240 ml) water over medium heat until the molasses has dissolved. Store the syrup in an airtight container in the fridge for up to 1 month.

HIBISCUS-CLOVE SYRUP

Makes 2 cups (480 ml)

It's easy to impart spice flavors to cocktail syrups and a great way to highlight and complement the inherent flavors in all the good booze you're using. This recipe is for the syrup used in our Union Street Collins cocktail (page 159). You can omit the hibiscus and swap out the cloves for cinnamon, cardamom, vanilla, etc., for endless variations.

1 cup (200 g) granulated sugar

¼ cup (8 g) dried hibiscus flowers

¼ teaspoon whole cloves

In a small saucepan, heat the sugar, hibiscus, and cloves with 1 cup (240 ml) water over low heat for 10 minutes, until the sugar has dissolved and the syrup has reduced by about one-quarter. Remove from the heat; strain and discard the solids. Store the syrup in an airtight container in the fridge for up to 1 month.

TEA SYRUP

Makes 2 cups (480 ml)

The delicious herbal flavors of teas find a great home in many cocktails, especially punches and anything with gin and citrus. This recipe is for a black tea syrup, but you can substitute anything you like, from green tea to Earl Grey to chai to peppermint!

1 cup (200 g) granulated or demerara sugar

2 tablespoons loose-leaf black tea

In a small saucepan, heat the sugar with 1 cup (240 ml) water over medium heat until the sugar has dissolved. Remove from the heat, stir in the tea, and let it steep for 5 minutes. Strain and discard the tea leaves. Store the syrup in an airtight container in the fridge for up to 1 month.

GRENADINE

Makes 4 cups (960 ml)

This recipe borrows heavily from Jeffrey Morgenthaler's classic reference (if you're unfamiliar with this gentleman and have any interest in cocktails whatsoever, I exhort you to get a copy of *The Bar Book*!). We add a little lemon juice for brightness and some spice, as well. This is incredibly easy, and you can make it with either fresh-squeezed or store-bought pomegranate juice. Your Shirley Temples will never be the same!

2 cups (480 ml) pure, unsweetened pomegranate juice

2 cups (400 g) sugar

1 cinnamon stick

2 whole cloves

1/4 cup (60 ml) pomegranate molasses

1 tablespoon fresh lemon juice

1 teaspoon orange blossom water

1 ounce (30 ml) vodka (optional preservative; if you'll use up all the grenadine in 1 month, you can skip it)

In a medium saucepan, heat the pomegranate juice, sugar, cinnamon, and cloves over medium heat until the sugar has just dissolved. Allow the spices to steep for about 30 minutes to impart the flavors to the syrup, then remove the whole spices and stir in the molasses, lemon juice, orange blossom water, and vodka (if using). Transfer the grenadine to a clean, airtight glass bottle and keep it in the fridge for up to 2 months.

ORGEAT

Makes 3 cups (720 ml)

The backbone of many great Tiki drinks (a mai tai is no mai tai without it!), orgeat—almond-flavored syrup—is often thought of as an intimidating ingredient that is not to be tried at home. We're really not sure why, as it's pretty simple to make, and homemade orgeat is miles better than the store-bought stuff. We tested a ton of recipes before landing on this one, which is inspired by the orgeat they make at Death & Co., a legendary cocktail haven in NYC.

1 cup (140 g) raw whole almonds

2 cups plus 2 tablespoons (270 ml) filtered water

1¼ cups (250 g) sugar

½ ounce vodka

¼ teaspoon orange blossom water

In a dry saucepan, toast the almonds over medium heat, stirring constantly, until they are golden brown and fragrant. Transfer them to a blender, add the water, and process for 2 minutes. Strain the mixture through a cheesecloth-lined sieve, squeezing out all the liquid.

In a medium saucepan, combine the almond milk and sugar. Cook them over medium heat, stirring and without boiling, until the sugar is dissolved. Remove the pan from the heat and stir in the vodka and orange blossom water. Store the orgeat in a clean, airtight glass bottle in the fridge for up to 1 month.

PRO TIP: **Make extra toasted almond milk to stir into your morning coffee; it's crazy delicious stuff.**

INFUSIONS

Infusions are another one of those fancy bartender tricks that seem
complex and intimidating, but are in fact incredibly easy.
Generally as simple as combining one ingredient with another and letting
time do the work, infusions add depth of flavor to a variety of cocktails
and are a great way to preserve seasonal ingredients. If you're
in a hurry, we've also got a method for quickly infusing flavor into spirits.
Infusions of dry ingredients such as spices, teas, and dried fruits
or vegetables will keep for months. Infusions with fresh fruits
and vegetables have a shorter shelf life, and should be refrigerated
and consumed within 1 month.

Basic Infusion

Take about a handful of the ingredient of your choice (chile peppers, lemon rinds, cherries, cocoa nibs, coffee—like we do for the Disco Nap (page 218), and put it into a bottle of the spirit of your choice (for a pure infusion without any competing flavors from the spirit, go with a high-proof vodka). Let it sit for any-where from 2 days to 2 months—the longer it infuses, the more potent the extraction. (P.S.: This is how you make homemade vanilla extract!) Just taste it every so often until it's where you want it, then strain out the solids and enjoy!

Quick Infusion

Using a blender, combine the spirit and the ingredient you want to infuse (this works best with fresh ingredients like lemongrass, ginger, or peppers). Blend on high speed until the ingredients have mostly broken down, then strain and discard the solids. We find it's best to refrigerate these infusions after they've been made, to maintain freshness.

FAT-WASHING

It's no surprise that the owners of a bar and bakery called Butter & Scotch are into adding fat to cocktails! The way to do that, known in the biz as "fat-washing," is as simple as Basic Infusion (at left), with one extra step. It really does impart the richness and flavor of whatever fat you use (bacon, peanut butter, brown butter, sesame oil) to the spirit, without any greasiness left behind.

Here's a recipe for Brown Butter Scotch, which we use in the Rita & Bernie (page 195). This is the basic technique, so play around with different spirits and fats (peanut butter and bourbon, anyone?), and make some magic! The butter takes on great Scotch flavor as well; try it in our Salted Chocolate Chip Cookies (page 168)!

Brown Butter Scotch

In a small saucepan, melt the butter over medium heat until it froths and milk solids start to brown on the bottom of the pan. Let them get nice and toasty (you'll smell a gorgeous nutty aroma), then remove from the heat (it can burn quickly, so pay attention!).

Combine the Scotch and melted butter in a wide-mouth airtight jar and give it a shake. Let it sit at room temperature for at least 1 hour, then freeze it for another hour (or longer).

Once the butter has risen to the top and frozen, use a knife or spoon to break it up. Pour the liquid through a coffee filter into an airtight container. Reserve the butter for another use (it's great on popcorn!). It will keep, wrapped and refrigerated, for up to 1 month. The brown butter scotch will keep for up to 6 months in the refrigerator.

1 cup (2 sticks / 225 g) unsalted butter

8 ounces (240 ml) single-malt Scotch (we like Macallan 12 for this, but anything that's not intensely peaty will work well)

Makes 1 cup (240 ml)

Brunch

Ah, brunch, the most **polarizing** of meals. It seems that it's a love-it-or-hate-it proposition. Some love the idea of **eating** and drinking the day away, while others prefer to lead productive lives on the weekend. We'll let you guess which category we fall into.

Our **brunch** menu at Butter & Scotch is a bit atypical for a bar/bakery, as it's almost exclusively made up of **biscuits**: lots of stuff piled on top of our insanely buttery, big-ass biscuits. So you won't find omelets or waffles or French toast or pancakes. You'll find a lot of biscuits. Oh, and **Magic Buns**, which you'll read about later. It's simple, but it works, because our biscuits are the best.

And lest you forget, we're a bar, and bars serve **booze**, and brunch booze is fun booze, so we've got Heirloom Bloody Marys and hangover-eradicating Micheladas and super-butch **Manmosas** for all you day-drinking enthusiasts. Just schedule time for a **nap** after!

Magic Buns

These buns owe a lot to the deservedly iconic Morning Buns at Tartine Bakery in San Francisco. Allison braved their inevitable line for one of the buns a few years back, and her mind was blown by the shattering, perfectly laminated pastry and the fresh aroma of orange zest. The technique for ours differs (but they're both laminated, which means the dough has been folded repeatedly, creating fluffy, buttery layers), and we add some Chinese five-spice mix for a little hint of anise, but we hope you'll find the end result to be just as magical as her memory of that chilly San Francisco morning.

Make the dough: In a microwave or on the stove, slightly warm up the milk. Add the yeast and allow it to bloom for 5 minutes.

In a large bowl, combine the milk and yeast mixture, half of the flour, 2 tablespoons of the sugar, and the eggs. Mix with a spatula until combined. Cover with a clean cloth and set aside.

In the bowl of a mixer fitted with the paddle attachment, combine the 2 cups (455 g) butter, ½ cup (65 g) of the flour, and 1 teaspoon of the salt. Beat on low speed until fully homogeneous. Turn the butter mixture out onto plastic wrap, form it into an 8-inch (20-cm) square, and wrap and refrigerate for at least 30 minutes.

Wipe out the mixer bowl and pour the yeast mixture (also known as the "sponge") into the bowl. Add the remaining 3 tablespoons sugar, 2½ cups (315 g) flour, 2 tablespoons salt, the vanilla, and the melted butter. Mix on low speed with the paddle attachment until incorporated, then turn the dough out onto a clean, lightly floured work surface and knead it for 5 minutes. Form it into a square, wrap it in plastic, and refrigerate for 30 minutes.

For the dough:

- 1¾ cups (420 ml) whole milk
- 2¼ teaspoons active dry yeast
- 6 cups (750 g) unbleached all-purpose flour
- 5 tablespoons (63 g) sugar, plus more for coating the pan and dusting
- 2 large eggs
- 2 cups (4 sticks / 455 g) unsalted butter, plus 2 tablespoons melted and more for greasing the pan
- 2 tablespoons plus 1 teaspoon kosher salt
- 1 teaspoon vanilla extract

For the filling:

- 1½ cups (330 g) firmly packed dark brown sugar
- 1½ tablespoons ground Chinese five-spice
- Zest of 1 orange
- 1½ tablespoons triple sec or orange liqueur
- Pinch of salt

RECIPE CONTINUES

Makes
12
buns

Roll the dough out to a 20 by 20-inch (50 by 50-cm) square. Lay the butter square in the center in a diamond shape. Fold the dough inward to encapsulate the butter. Press the edges together to seal them, wrap the package in plastic, and return it to the fridge for 30 minutes.

Place the chilled dough on a lightly floured surface and, using a heavy rolling pin, pound it a few times to make it more pliable. Roll it out to a 20 by 10-inch (50 by 25-cm) rectangle. Fold it into thirds, like folding a business letter. Rotate the dough packet one-quarter turn to the right, then repeat the rolling and folding. Wrap and refrigerate it for another 30 minutes, and repeat the rolling and folding with another two turns. Wrap and refrigerate the dough for 30 minutes more.

Grease a muffin pan and dust the cups with sugar.

Make the filling: In a medium bowl, mix together the brown sugar, five-spice, orange zest, triple sec or orange liqueur, and salt to combine.

On a lightly floured surface, roll the dough out to a 15 by 20-inch (38 by 50-cm) rectangle, then spread on the filling mixture, leaving a ½-inch (12-mm) margin clear. Roll it up lengthwise into a 20-inch (50-cm) long tube. Cut the tube into 12 equal slices. Lay the pieces swirl side up in the muffin cups. Allow the buns to proof by setting them aside, covered loosely in plastic wrap, in a warm place until they're doubled in size, 30 to 45 minutes.

Preheat the oven to 350°F (175°C). Bake the buns for 25 to 30 minutes, rotating them once halfway through, until they're golden brown, flaky, and caramelized. Immediately flip them out onto a clean tray and roll in more sugar. Shake off excess sugar and serve immediately. (These buns are magical when fresh, but after a day, they become stale, even when stored in an airtight container. If you're going to go through the effort of making them, eat them at their best!)

MAGIC BUNS CONTINUED

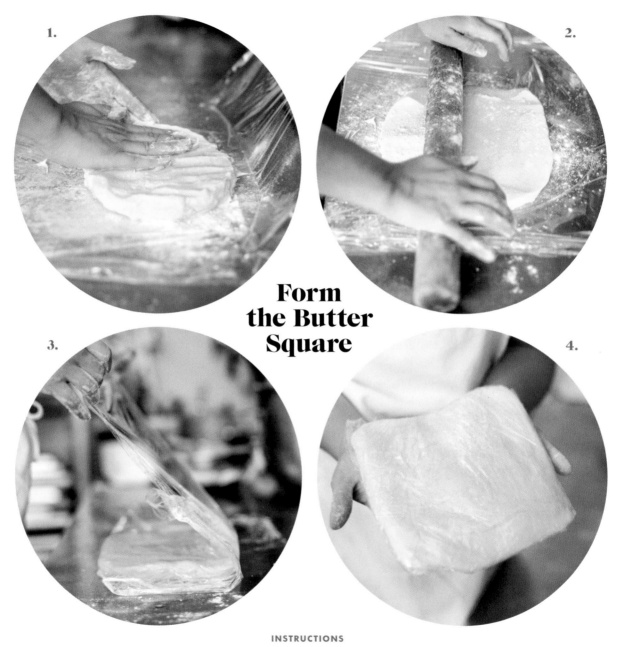

Form the Butter Square

INSTRUCTIONS

1. Turn the butter and flour mixture out onto plastic wrap.

2. Roll the mixture out into an 8-inch (20-cm) square. \ 3. Wrap well with plastic.

4. Refrigerate for at least 30 minutes.

1.

2.

Create the Dough Envelope

3.

4.

INSTRUCTIONS

1. Remove the dough from the refrigerator and roll it out . . .
2. . . . into a 20 by 20-inch (50 by 50-cm) square. \ 3. Lay the butter square
in the center of the dough in a diamond shape. Fold the edges of the dough
inward to meet in the middle and envelop the butter. \ 4. Press the edges together to
seal them, wrap in plastic, and refrigerate for 30 minutes.

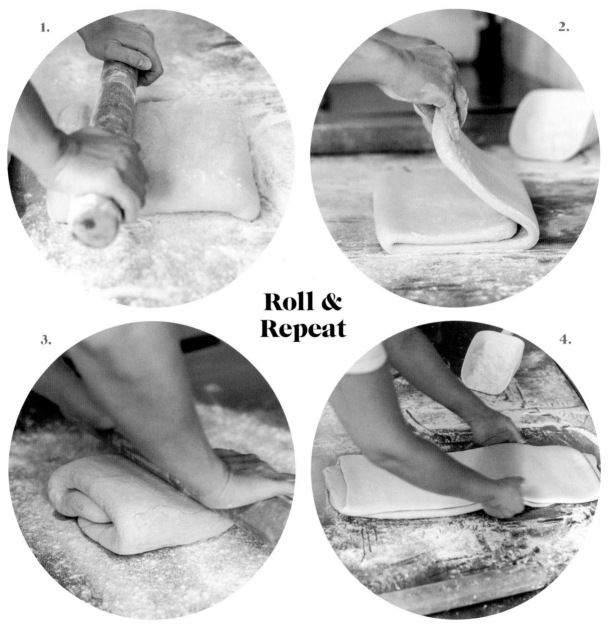

1.

2.

Roll & Repeat

3.

4.

INSTRUCTIONS

1. On a lightly floured surface, pound the dough with a rolling pin a few times to make it pliable. Roll the square out to a 10 by 20-inch (25 by 50-cm) rectangle. \ 2. Fold the bottom third of the rectangle up to the center, then the top third over it, as if you're folding a business letter. \ 3. Turn the packet one-quarter to the right, and roll again . . . \ 4. . . . into a 10 by 20-inch (25 by 50-cm) rectangle, then fold the envelope once more. Wrap in plastic and refrigerate for 30 minutes.

Fill & Assemble

1. Roll out the dough, then spread it evenly with the filling mixture, leaving a ½-inch (12-mm) margin clear. \ 2. Roll it up lengthwise into a 20-inch (50-cm) long tube. \ 3. Cut the tube into 12 slices approximately 1½ inches (4 cm) thick. 4. Lay the pieces swirl side up in the muffin pans.

1.

2.

Bake & Sugar

3.

4.

INSTRUCTIONS

1. Allow the buns to proof: Set them aside, covered loosely in plastic wrap,
in a warm place until they've doubled in size, 30 to 45 minutes.
2. After baking, flip the buns out onto a clean tray . . . \ 3. . . . and roll them in more
sugar. \ 4. Shake off any excess sugar and serve immediately.

Apple-Cheddar Turnovers

The first time Allison heard that some people enjoy Cheddar cheese on top of their apple pie, she was just a kid, with a very limited palate, and her first reaction was, "Huh?!" As she got older and her tastes became more sophisticated, she soon learned to appreciate this American diner staple. The sharp creaminess of the Cheddar is a great savory foil to the sweet and tart apple filling, and that sweet-savory contrast is especially appropriate at brunch time. This is basically a portable version of that slice of pie—whip up a bunch and enjoy them on the go or at your breakfast table with a cup of coffee, some morning sunlight, and something great on the stereo.

At the final stage of preparing the pie crust, before wrapping it in plastic to rest, mix ½ cup (55 g) of the shredded cheese in with the dough mixture. Then proceed as instructed.

While the dough is chilling, make the filling: In a large mixing bowl, combine the brown sugar, cornstarch, ginger, cinnamon, and salt. Add the apples and toss them with the sugar-spice mixture.

Preheat the oven to 375°F (190°C).

RECIPE CONTINUES

1 recipe All-Butter Pie Crust (page 34), with cheese added just before the final step (see instructions)

1 cup (115 g) shredded sharp Cheddar cheese

½ cup (110 g) firmly packed dark brown sugar

1 tablespoon cornstarch

½ teaspoon ground ginger

½ teaspoon ground cinnamon

½ teaspoon kosher salt

2 pounds (910 g) firm, tart apples (Granny Smith, Mutsu, and Macoun are all good choices), cut into ½-inch (12-mm) cubes

1 large egg

¼ cup (60 ml) whole milk or water

Raw sugar, for sprinkling

Makes
4
turnovers

After the dough has chilled, allow it to rest for about 5 minutes at room temperature to soften up. Divide it into quarters, and roll out each quarter on a lightly floured surface into a round 5 to 6 inches (12 to 15 cm) in diameter and about ¼ inch (6 mm) thick. Spoon the apple filling into the center of each dough round, being careful not to overfill.

In a small bowl, whisk together the egg and milk or water to make an egg wash. Use the egg wash to wet the outer edge of each round, then fold one side of the dough over the filling to meet the other edge, and press gently with the tines of a fork all the way around to seal.

Transfer the turnovers to a parchment-lined baking sheet. Using a paring knife, cut one or two steam vents into the top of each turnover. Brush each with egg wash and sprinkle with raw sugar and the remaining ½ cup (55 g) Cheddar cheese.

Bake for 20 minutes, rotating once halfway through, then lower the heat to 350°F (175°C) and bake for another 20 minutes, or until the crust is golden brown and the juices bubbling up have thickened. Remove the turnovers to a wire rack to cool. Serve them warm or at room temperature. The turnovers will keep in an airtight container in the refrigerator for up to 5 days. To reheat, warm them in a preheated 350°F (175°C) oven or toaster oven for 5 minutes.

Allison's Oatmeal

Much as we'd love to eat buttery biscuits and sweet pastries for breakfast every day, we recognize the need for the occasional nod at nutrition. That's where Allison's (admittedly weird) oatmeal comes in. She's not a big fan of the classic oatmeal situation, with fruit and nuts and milk and all that. She prefers to go savory and spicy, with some peanut butter for protein. It may sound odd to you, but give it a try, and make your Goody Two-Shoes breakfast choice a bit more interesting!

½ cup (45 g) rolled oats

1 tablespoon natural peanut butter (creamy or smooth, up to you!)

½ teaspoon sriracha hot sauce (How much heat can you handle? Adjust accordingly.)

½ teaspoon kosher salt

Bring 1 cup (240 ml) water to a boil. Stir in the oats and cook for about 5 minutes, or until creamy. While the oatmeal is still hot, stir in the peanut butter, hot sauce, and salt. Eat it!

Serves 1

BROOKLYN
BISCUITS

1.

2.

3.

Brooklyn Biscuits

When approaching the daunting task of creating a biscuit for our shop, we knew what we wanted the end result to be, but we weren't sure how to get there. We approached our baker, Lindsey, with our dilemma, and she immediately reached into her bag, pulled out a small recipe book she had been creating over the years, and quietly whispered to me, as if she were confessing her darkest secret, "I have the Popeye's recipe."

The Popeye's recipe created a tasty but thin disk-like biscuit, and we wanted something bigger and fluffier. We cut out all the shortening from the recipe and replaced it with butter to give our biscuits more of that buttery flavor we wanted. We also took out the milk powder, which added a milky flavor but created a dense, dry texture. And we used heavy cream curdled with some apple cider vinegar instead of buttermilk because of its higher fat content.

After a bit more tweaking here and there, we had found it. It looks nothing like a Popeye's biscuit, but it's the biscuit of our dreams: It's got a firm but flaky exterior and is fluffy, dense, and buttery inside. It's so good that now everything but two items on our brunch menu is served on this biscuit.

- 2½ cups (600 ml) heavy cream
- 2 teaspoons apple cider vinegar
- 4½ cups (565 g) unbleached all-purpose flour, plus more for dusting
- 1 tablespoon plus 2 teaspoons baking powder
- 2 teaspoons kosher salt
- 2 teaspoons sugar
- 1 teaspoon baking soda
- 1 cup (2 sticks / 225 g) cold unsalted butter, chopped into ½-inch (12-mm) pieces

Preheat the oven to 350°F (175°C).

In a small bowl, mix together the cream and vinegar and set aside.

In the bowl of a stand mixer fitted with the paddle attachment, combine the flour, baking powder, salt, sugar, and baking soda and mix on low. Add the butter and mix on medium-low speed until the butter is broken down to small, pea-size pieces. Turn the mixer back to low and slowly add the cream and vinegar mixture. Mix just until the dough comes together. Do not overmix, or the biscuits will be tough.

Pour the dough onto a floured surface and pat it down until it's about 2 inches (5 cm) thick. Use a 3-inch (7.5-cm) cookie or biscuit cutter to cut out eight rounds. Arrange the rounds on a parchment-lined baking sheet. Pat together the scraps and cut out more rounds if possible; you should be able to get another biscuit or two. Be gentle so the biscuits don't get tough. Discard any remaining scraps.

Bake the biscuits for 15 to 20 minutes, or until they are golden brown. Remove them to a wire rack, then serve warm. Store leftovers in an airtight container at room temperature for up to 2 days.

PRO TIP: After you cut out the rounds of dough, you can freeze them for a few months and bake them when needed. The baking time for frozen biscuits is closer to 35 minutes.

Makes
8 to **10**
biscuits

Deli-Style Bacon, Egg & Cheese

We took inspiration from the many bodegas around New York who keep hungover New Yorkers alive with their egg and cheese sandwiches when we were figuring out the method for scrambling our eggs for these. The first step is to use a large skillet. This allows the eggs to spread out very thin like a crêpe so you can fold them into a cute little envelope before placing it on your sandwich. Step two is to use at least 1 tablespoon of butter for every batch so that the pretty little egg envelope doesn't stick when transferring it to the sandwich. This method will ensure that when a bite is taken, egg bits don't go falling everywhere as they would using the traditional scramble method.

2 large eggs

Kosher salt and freshly ground black pepper

1 Brooklyn Biscuit (page 74)

1 slice sharp Cheddar cheese

1 tablespoon unsalted butter

2 strips bacon, cooked

Hot sauce, for serving

Preheat the oven to 350°F (175°C).

In a small bowl, beat the eggs with a generous amount of salt and pepper. Set aside.

Cut the biscuit in half and place the cheese on one side of the biscuit. Pop the biscuit in the oven to melt the cheese.

While the cheese is melting, melt the butter in a large sauté pan over medium heat. Pour in the eggs and let them spread out in a thin layer; wait for them to form a crêpelike pancake. The instant the eggs are cooked through (about 30 seconds), fold the edges inward with a spatula and transfer the eggs to the cheese side of the biscuit. Top with the bacon and other half of the biscuit to create a sandwich. Serve immediately, with hot sauce on the side.

Serves 1

Biscuits & Gravy

There are not many things more comforting than piping hot gravy poured over biscuits. We tell ourselves every weekend that we're going to abstain from the stuff, but every time we walk through the door on Saturday morning to smell the sausage sizzling in the skillet, we lose all willpower.

We keep this recipe simple to allow the flavor of the sausage to be the star of the dish—so look for good-quality sausage. We suggest trying your local butcher shop. We also use bacon fat in our gravy, but if you don't have that lying around, butter will do the trick!

If you want a vegetarian version, we also serve a mushroom gravy, which is given as a variation, opposite.

1 pound (455 g) loose sweet Italian sausage

1 tablespoon bacon fat or butter

¼ cup (30 g) unbleached all-purpose flour

2 cups (480 ml) whole milk

Kosher salt and freshly ground black pepper

4 Brooklyn Biscuits (page 70), warmed

In a saucepan over medium-high heat, brown the sausage until it's fully cooked. Add the bacon fat or butter and flour and mix with a wooden spoon or spatula, making sure it doesn't burn on the bottom. After 30 seconds, add the milk. Stir, scraping up the bits from the bottom of the saucepan, then bring the gravy to a boil and let it simmer until the mixture thickens to the desired consistency. Season to taste with salt and pepper.

Split the biscuits in half and lay them open-faced onto plates. Spoon the gravy on top and serve.

Serves 4

MUSHROOM GRAVY

Makes 4 cups (960 ml); serves 4

In a saucepan, melt 2 tablespoons of the butter. Add the mushrooms and salt and sauté until the mushrooms have let out their juices and are slightly browned. Add the remaining 2 tablespoons butter and the flour and mix with a wooden spoon or spatula, making sure it doesn't burn on the bottom. After 30 seconds, add the milk. Stir, scraping up the bits from the bottom of the saucepan, then bring the gravy to a boil and let simmer until the mixture thickens to the desired consistency. Season to taste with salt and pepper.

¼ cup (½ stick / 55 g) unsalted butter

Kosher salt

1 pound (455 g) thinly sliced mushrooms (we use a mix of white button and cremini)

¼ cup (30 g) unbleached all-purpose flour

2½ cups (600 ml) whole milk

Freshly ground black pepper

BLT

Full disclosure: Keavy's never been a big fan of ordering BLTs. They're always served on dry wheat toast and never have as much mayo as she prefers (however, she probably prefers more than the average person). Turns out, when you sub out the wheat toast for a buttery biscuit, use thick-cut good-quality bacon, and use romaine lettuce instead iceberg, it makes a pretty big difference.

1 Brooklyn Biscuit (page 74)

1 tablespoon mayonnaise

3 slices fresh tomato

Kosher salt and freshly ground black pepper

3 strips thick-cut bacon, cooked crispy

1 leaf romaine lettuce

Carefully slice the biscuit in half. Spread mayo on both sides of the biscuit. Place the tomatoes on the bottom side of the biscuit. Season them with salt and pepper. Break the strips of bacon in half and place them on top of the tomatoes. Tear up the romaine leaf and place it on the top side of the biscuit, "gluing" it to the biscuit with the mayo. Close the sandwich and enjoy!

Serves 1

Sweet & Savory

The idea for this came from a deluxe pancake meal from the local diner: stacks of pancakes smeared with cinnamon butter and maple syrup with a side of bacon and eggs. Here, we subbed out the pancakes for our biscuits and tossed everything together into a sandwich.

Preheat the oven to 350°F (175°C).

In a small bowl, combine the butter and cinnamon to create a spreadable mixture. Carefully cut the biscuit in half and pop it in the oven for 5 five minutes to heat it up. While this is happening, fry the egg to your preferred level of runniness, making sure to salt and pepper it well. Spread the cinnamon butter onto both halves of the biscuit. Add a small pinch of kosher salt. Top one half with bacon and the fried egg. Cover it with the other biscuit half to make a tall sandwich and then pour the maple syrup over the top.

Serves 1

3 tablespoons unsalted butter, at room temperature

¼ teaspoon ground cinnamon

1 Brooklyn Biscuit (page 74)

1 large egg

Kosher salt and freshly ground black pepper

3 strips thick-cut bacon, cooked crispy

2 tablespoons real maple syrup

Smoked Trout Benedict

There used to be a restaurant in the West Village of NYC called the Grange, and back in Allison's early twenties, she would often sit at the bar and treat herself to their spread of smoked trout with rye toast, horseradish cream, and pickled red onion. It felt like a very adult indulgence, sitting alone at the bar in a beautiful restaurant, eating smoked fish (sometimes with a glass of Scotch on the side). This is a bit of an homage to that memory, made even richer with the addition of biscuits and poached eggs!

1 Brooklyn Biscuit (page 74)

1 smoked trout fillet (about 4 ounces / 115 g)

Pickled red onion (from Pickled Beets and Onions, page 114)

2 large eggs, poached (see Note)

½ cup (120 ml) Horseradish Hollandaise (opposite)

½ teaspoon caraway seeds

Open up the biscuit on a plate and top each half with smoked trout (tear it up a bit with your fingers). Pile on some pickled red onion (to taste) and top with the poached eggs. Spoon Horseradish Hollandaise on top and garnish with a sprinkling of caraway seeds. Serve immediately.

NOTE: Everyone seems to have their favorite egg-poaching method, and if you've got one you like, go with what you know! If you've never poached an egg before, and you're only doing a small number of them, we suggest Julia Child's foolproof method: Take 2 eggs, prick the bottom of each shell with a thumbtack or safety pin, and immerse them in simmering water for 10 seconds. Remove them from the water, bring it down to a gentle simmer, and crack the eggs into the water. Poach for 2 minutes, remove them with a slotted spoon, drain them for a moment on a paper towel, and serve.

Serves 1

HORSERADISH HOLLANDAISE

Makes 1½ cups (360 ml)

10 tablespoons (1¼ sticks / 140 g) unsalted butter
½ cup (125 g) freshly grated horseradish
3 large egg yolks
1 tablespoon fresh lemon juice
½ teaspoon salt
¼ teaspoon cayenne

In a small saucepan over medium heat, melt the butter. In a blender, combine the horseradish, egg yolks, lemon juice, salt, and cayenne and process on high speed. With the blender running, carefully add the hot melted butter to the mixture, pouring it in a thin stream. Continue to blend for 1 to 2 minutes, until the hollandaise is thick, creamy, and fully combined. Refrigerate leftover hollandaise in an airtight container for up to 1 week.

Strawberry Shortcake

On the sweeter side of the brunch spectrum, some go for waffles, while others dig pancakes, and French toast is the choice for some. We say you can keep 'em all; just give us some strawberry shortcake. Nothing beats the savory, buttery crumble of a freshly baked biscuit under an ethereal cloud of vanilla-scented whipped cream and fresh strawberries just beginning to release their juices. It is the perfect cross between breakfast and dessert.

1 cup (145 g) whole
  strawberries

4 tablespoons (50 g) sugar

1 cup (240 ml) heavy cream

1 teaspoon vanilla extract

1 Brooklyn Biscuit (page 74)

Hull and slice the strawberries (to hull the berries, use a paring knife to carefully cut out the green leaves and small core at the top of each berry). In a bowl, toss them with 3 tablespoons of the sugar and let them sit, covered, at room temperature for at least 10 minutes and up to 30 minutes.

In a separate bowl, whip the cream with the vanilla and remaining 1 tablespoon of sugar until soft peaks form.

Split open the biscuit on a plate, spoon over the berries and their juices, and top with the whipped cream. Serve immediately.

Serves 1

Yorkshire Popovers

If you're not familiar with popovers, we are happy to rectify that major omission from your culinary life! Popovers are hot, puffy pillows of delectable dough, and the perfect vehicle for all manner of deliciousness, from jam to gravy to honey to pretty much anything you want to put on them. These are sort of a cross between the justifiably famous popovers at Jordan Pond House in Maine, and the Yorkshire pudding that Allison's aunt and uncle make every year for Christmas. They usually serve it with rare roast beef, but we're putting a breakfast spin on it and serving it with some homemade jam. Eat these hot out of the oven!

- 1¾ cups (220 g) unbleached all-purpose flour
- ½ teaspoon kosher salt
- ⅛ teaspoon baking soda
- 3 large eggs
- 1 large egg white
- 2½ cups (600 ml) whole milk, plus more if needed
- Canola oil, for greasing the pan
- Homemade jam (see pages 88–92) and salted butter, for serving

Preheat the oven to 425°F (220°C).

Sift the flour, salt, and baking soda into a large bowl. Whisk in the eggs and egg white, then whisk in the milk. You should have a nice, thick batter that coats the back of a spoon. If it's too thick, add a bit more milk.

Generously grease a heavy-gauge muffin tin with canola oil and put it in the oven to heat until it's almost smoking, about 5 minutes. When it's hot, add the batter, filling each cavity almost to the top. Bake for about 30 minutes (without opening the oven door!), until the popovers have risen and are golden.

Remove the pan to a wire rack, and when cool enough to handle, serve the popovers with the jam and butter.

Makes

12

popovers

Strawberry-Basil Jam

We make a strawberry-basil pie every summer (the recipe for that is in Allison's other cookbook, *First Prize Pies*). This jam is a great way to capture the flavors of that pie and have them year-round! The more savory components in here balance beautifully with the bright, sweet strawberries and sugar.

In a large pot, combine the strawberries, basil, sugar, apple, vinegar, vanilla bean and seeds, lemon zest and juice, and pepper. Cover and let stand for anywhere from 30 minutes to overnight. In the meantime, if you plan to can the jam, prepare the jars and lids (see page 228).

Put a small plate in the freezer (we'll come back to this later).

Bring the jam mixture to a boil over medium-high heat, stirring often. Boil it hard, stirring frequently, until foam appears and then dissipates on the surface of the jam (this should take 15 to 20 minutes).

When the jam thickens, the bubbles will pop more slowly on the surface, and the mixture will slide off the surface of your spatula or spoon. At this point, pull it off the heat.

2 pounds (910 g) fresh strawberries, hulled and halved

10 large basil leaves, thinly sliced

2 cups (400 g) sugar

⅓ cup (55 g) finely grated peeled green apple

3 tablespoons high-quality balsamic vinegar

1 vanilla bean, split and scraped (see Note)

Zest and juice of 1 lemon

1 teaspoon freshly ground black pepper

Take 1 teaspoon of the mixture and put it on the surface of the plate you've been keeping in the freezer. Return the plate to the freezer for 2 minutes, then test it by pushing your finger against the edge of the jam on the plate. If it wrinkles up instead of letting your finger slide right through, it's ready. If not, return it to the heat and cook it until you get the results you want.

After the mixture has reached the right setting point, remove it from the heat and let it rest for about 5 minutes. Remove the vanilla bean.

Ladle the jam into hot, sterile jars, and if you're canning it, process them in a water bath. Otherwise, allow them cool to room temperature, then refrigerate. The jam will keep for up to 1 month in the fridge (but it won't last that long!).

Makes about 4 cups (960 ml)

NOTE: To get the most out of those expensive vanilla beans, split them lengthwise with a paring knife, and use the knife to scrape out the seeds from the inside. Use both the scraped bean and the seeds in the recipe, and remove the bean after it's prepared.

Winter Citrus Marmalade

This is a great way to preserve the beautiful, vibrant citrus of winter. Take advantage of the diverse range of winter citrus you can find—just keep the overall weight the same. Don't use limes, though; their leathery skins don't make good marmalade.

Cut the stem ends off the fruits, cut each fruit in half lengthwise, and remove the seeds. Using a vegetable slicer or mandoline, cut the halves into very thin half-moons (you can use a very sharp knife, but it's hard to get slices as uniform and thin as with a mandoline). Wrap the grated apple in cheesecloth and tie it into a tight bundle.

In a large pot, combine the citrus, sugar, lemon zest and juice, vanilla bean and seeds, and green apple sachet. Cover with 4 cups (960 ml) water and bring it to a boil over high heat. Lower the heat to maintain a strong simmer and cook, stirring frequently, about 40 minutes, or until the fruit is very soft.

While the fruit is cooking, prepare and sterilize your jars and lids (see page 228), and place a small plate in the freezer.

Remove the sachet from the pot, increase the heat to restore to a full boil, and cook until it reaches 220°F (105°C) on a candy thermometer, about 30 minutes. Remove the marmalade from the heat. Put 1 teaspoon of it on the plate in the freezer for 2 minutes, then test it by pushing your finger against the edge of the jam. If it wrinkles up instead of letting your finger slide through, it's ready. If not, return it to the heat and cook it until you get the results you want.

After the mixture reaches the setting point, remove it from the heat and let it rest for 5 minutes. Stir in the brandy (if using), then ladle the marmalade into hot, sterile jars and process them in a water bath, or allow them to come to room temperature, then refrigerate. The jam will keep for up to 1 month in the fridge.

2 pounds (910 g) mixed winter citrus fruits (we like kumquats, Meyer lemons, tangerines, and pomelos)

1 green apple, cored and grated

5 cups (1 kg) sugar

Zest and juice of 1 lemon

1 vanilla bean, split and scraped (see Note, page 89)

2 tablespoons brandy or cognac (optional)

Makes about 3 quarts (2.8 L)

Passion Fruit Curd

For our inaugural monthly pop-up dinner, we gave the wonderful and talented chef Shanna Pacifico command of our kitchen for an evening of small plates inspired by her take on Brazilian cuisine. We wanted to create a dessert to complement her flavors and came up with a passion fruit trifle. The passion fruit curd we made for it was so addictive—it's wonderful on its own and the perfect thing to slather over a warm popover (page 86) for a little burst of the tropics! If you're unfamiliar with fruit curds, they're a delicious way to transform sour ingredients like citrus juice into a creamy, buttery spread that still keeps the bright tartness of the fruit.

2 cups (400 g) sugar

2 cups (480 ml) passion fruit puree (see Note)

8 large egg yolks

1 teaspoon kosher salt

½ cup (1 stick / 115 g) unsalted butter, cut into chunks

Bring about 1 inch (2.5 cm) of water to a boil over medium-high heat in a saucepan. In a medium-size glass or metal bowl that will fit over the saucepan without the bottom touching the water, whisk together the sugar, fruit puree, egg yolks, and salt. Whisk continuously until you see whisk marks appearing in the curd and it thickens enough to coat the back of a spoon.

Remove the curd from the heat and whisk in the butter. Immediately strain the curd through a fine-mesh sieve to remove any clumps and allow it to cool before putting it in a clean, covered container. The curd will keep in the fridge for up to 2 weeks.

NOTE: You can find passion fruit puree in the freezer section of some specialty grocers, but if you want to make your own, you'll need 40 to 50 ripe passion fruits. Cut them in half, scoop the flesh and seeds into a large pot, and cook very gently over low heat with 1 teaspoon of water per fruit (about 1 cup / 240 ml total). Remove the pot from the heat and puree the mixture on low in a blender for about 10 seconds. Press it through a fine-mesh strainer to remove the seeds. The puree can be refrigerated for up to 3 days or frozen for up to 3 months.

Makes about 5 cups (1.2 L)

Granola

With *butter* in our name, it's no surprise that most of our baked goods are a bit dairy heavy. This recipe, however, is flavorful and rich and completely dairy free! We use pecans and dried cherries, but you can add any kind of dried fruit and nut to make this recipe your own.

Preheat the oven to 350°F (175°C).

In a large bowl, combine the oats, pecans, coconut, brown sugar, oil, syrup, vanilla, salt, cinnamon, and ginger and toss to mix thoroughly. Spread them onto a parchment-lined large rimmed baking sheet and bake for 20 to 25 minutes, tossing every 5 minutes so that everything toasts evenly. Let the granola cool. Add the dried cherries and give it all a good toss. Serve with milk or yogurt. Keep the granola in an airtight container for up to 2 months.

Serves 6

2 cups (180 g) rolled oats

1 cup (120 g) chopped pecans

½ cup (45 g) unsweetened coconut flakes

½ cup (110 g) firmly packed dark brown sugar

½ cup (120 ml) canola oil

1 tablespoon real maple syrup

½ teaspoon vanilla extract

½ teaspoon kosher salt

⅛ teaspoon ground cinnamon

Pinch dried ground ginger

¼ cup (35 g) dried cherries

Rhonda's Green Chile Cornbread

Allison loves collecting vintage cookbooks, and some of her favorites are from her own childhood. Her mom, Rhonda, contributed recipes to some of the floppy, spiral-bound tomes produced by her elementary and middle schools, and to this day she references them when looking for culinary inspiration. One of our go-tos is Rhonda's cornbread, which is a key component of our Kings County Corn Bowl Sundae (page 123). Spiked with Hatch green chiles from New Mexico (where Allison was born), and whole corn kernels for texture and sweetness, it's the best we've ever had!

Preheat the oven to 375°F (190°C).

Butter a 9-inch (23-cm) square baking dish or a 9-inch (23-cm) cast-iron skillet and set aside.

In a large bowl, whisk together the flour, cornmeal, sugar, baking powder, and salt. In a separate small bowl, beat the egg and milk together, then add them to the dry ingredients along with the 2 tablespoons melted butter, the corn kernels, and chiles. Stir well, then spread the batter into the buttered baking dish. Bake for 30 to 35 minutes, or until lightly browned around the edges. Serve warm, slathered with more butter!

Serves 8 to 12

2 tablespoons butter, melted, plus extra for the baking dish

1¼ cups (155 g) unbleached all-purpose flour

¾ cup (135 g) fine cornmeal

¼ cup (50 g) sugar

1 tablespoon plus 2 teaspoons baking powder

1 teaspoon kosher salt

1 large egg

½ cup (120 ml) milk

½ cup (80 g) fresh or frozen corn kernels

½ cup (100 g) diced green chiles (we use frozen chopped hot Hatch chiles, but if you use canned, drain, rinse, and add ¼ teaspoon cayenne)

Mama T's Tuna Quiche

The first time I tried a traditional quiche, I was confused. I didn't understand how that could be a quiche. Where was the starchy texture? The gooey chunks of Swiss? And most important, where was the tuna? Of all my mom's retro/nostalgic recipes, her quiche was my favorite. This is what I requested as my last meal before going to summer camp and my first meal back from a college break. To me it tastes like home. When I met Keavy and Allison and learned of their plans to have weekend brunch, I knew that they had to try my mother's tuna quiche. Much to their surprise, they loved it as much as my three siblings and I do, and immediately added it to our opening brunch menu. Being able to share Mama T's quiche with the lovely Butter & Scotch ladies has been a welcome taste of my childhood kitchen. — *Lindsey Thalheimer, Former Kitchen Manager*

½ recipe All-Butter Pie Crust (page 34)

½ cup (120 ml) mayonnaise

½ cup (120 ml) whole milk

2 large eggs

2 tablespoons unbleached all-purpose flour

6 ounces (170 g) Swiss cheese, cubed

1 (5-ounce / 142-g) can tuna packed in water, drained

⅓ cup (50 g) sliced Kalamata olives

¼ cup (15 g) thinly sliced scallions

1½ teaspoons Dijon mustard

Pinch of cayenne

Preheat the oven to 350°F (175°C).

On a lightly floured work surface, roll out the butter crust and fit it into an 8-inch (20-cm) springform cake pan. Refrigerate until ready to use. In a large bowl, beat together the mayonnaise, milk, eggs, and flour. Add the cheese, tuna, olives, scallions, mustard, and cayenne to the egg mixture and stir well. Pour all of the ingredients into the chilled butter crust and bake for 20 to 25 minutes, until the top is golden brown and the center has set. Allow the quiche to cool for at least 20 minutes, then serve it warm or at room temperature. Leftovers can be kept in the fridge for up to 1 week and warmed in a 350°F (175°C) oven for 15 minutes.

Maple-Bacon Cupcakes

This is by far our number one bestselling cupcake, and for good reason: It's a delicious cake made with tons of real maple syrup and a hefty amount of cinnamon, plus it's topped with vanilla frosting, a large cut of bacon, and a pinch of kosher salt. Keavy came up with it in 2009, back when bacon on a cupcake was unheard of. People caught on, and now you can find at least one bacon cupcake at almost every local cupcake shop. And because there's maple syrup and bacon involved, it's absolutely acceptable to eat this cupcake for breakfast!

1½ cups (190 g) unbleached all-purpose flour

1 teaspoon baking powder

½ teaspoon kosher salt, plus more for topping

¾ cup (150 g) sugar

1 cup (2 sticks / 225 g) unsalted butter, melted

4 large eggs

⅓ cup (80 ml) real maple syrup

2 teaspoons vanilla extract

1 teaspoon ground cinnamon

Keavy's Favorite Vanilla Frosting (page 28)

8 strips thick-cut bacon, cooked crispy

Preheat the oven to 350°F (175°C). Line mini-cupcake pans with paper liners. (The batter is too dense and rich for large cupcakes.) In a large bowl, combine the flour, baking powder, and salt and set aside.

In the bowl of a stand mixer fitted with the whisk attachment, combine the sugar and butter. Mix on medium speed for about 1 minute to cool the butter. Add the eggs, maple syrup, vanilla, and cinnamon all at once, and mix until fully incorporated. Turn the speed down to low and add the flour mixture. Mix just until the batter becomes smooth. Do not turn the mixer to high speed, or it will overwork the flour and will create a drier cupcake.

Spoon the batter into the cupcake pans and bake for 8 to 10 minutes, until just risen and a cake tester comes out clean. Let the cupcakes cool completely before frosting.

Top each cupcake with vanilla frosting, about 1 inch (2.5 cm) of bacon, and a pinch of kosher salt. Store, covered, at room temperature for no more than 1 day.

Makes 4 dozen mini-cupcakes

Manmosa

Keavy's first time making a Manmosa was around 11 A.M. on the Metro-North after a pretty rough night. She grabbed an overpriced Bud Light from one of the beer vendors in Grand Central Station, got some Tropicana orange juice, and had herself a lovely morning cocktail on her train ride to upstate New York.

The version below is the traditional one, using Miller High Life ("The Champagne of Beers") instead of Bud Light, as well as fresh-squeezed OJ, which makes all the difference. If you want to get a little fancy with it, you could even substitute in a white ale or, for a bit of bitterness, an IPA.

1 (12-ounce / 355-ml) bottle Miller High Life, cold

¼ cup (60 ml) fresh orange juice, pulp strained

Fill a pint glass three-quarters full with beer, then fill it the rest of the way with orange juice. Enjoy!

Serves 1

Crown Heights Coffee

This is a little homage to Brooklyn, incorporating iced coffee with Hennessy cognac (very popular in our neighborhood) and Black Chocolate Stout from our friends at Brooklyn Brewery. It's a refreshing, updated take on the classic Irish coffee, and it's delicious!

Combine the coffee, stout, cognac, and syrup in a Collins glass and fill it with ice. Pour in the heavy cream and sprinkle some cocoa powder on top. Serve!

NOTE: Cold-brew coffee is all the rage these days, and it can be delicious. That said, we like a little more depth and darkness to our iced coffee, so we use a Japanese method of brewing hot coffee directly onto ice. This cools the coffee down fast, capturing flavors and aromatics you'd lose if you just let hot coffee come to room temperature. The pour-over method is easiest, but you could also put the ice in your coffee pot and brew directly onto that in a traditional coffee brewer.

For 2 cups (480 ml) of iced coffee, put ½ pound (225 g) ice in a heat-safe glass vessel, top it with a pour-over cone, add a filter and 1 ounce (28 g) ground coffee, then pour over 1 cup (240 ml) boiling water. That's it! You now have delicious, strong iced coffee.

Serves 1

2 ounces (60 ml) strong iced coffee (see Note)

2 ounces (60 ml) Brooklyn Brewery Black Chocolate Stout or dark stout beer of your choice

2 ounces (60 ml) Hennessy V.S Cognac or cognac of your choice

½ ounce Simplest Simple Syrup (page 47)

Ice cubes

¾ ounce heavy cream

Unsweetened cocoa powder, for garnish

Pepsi Milk

People often ask why we serve Pepsi instead of Coke. In NYC restaurants, it's a somewhat unorthodox decision. The reason is simple: Allison grew up in a Pepsi family. Her dad, and his dad before him, drove a Pepsi truck through Brooklyn for many years. Growing up, she had a fridge in her garage that was exclusively stocked with Pepsi and its affiliated soda brands, as special treats for guests and parties (Allison's mom would rarely let her kids touch the stuff!). When her dad was a kid, his parents used to make him and his sister drink Pepsi milk every morning, and as a result, they both grew up hating it. It sounds utterly bizarre, and it's just what it sounds like: milk and Pepsi mixed together. But somehow, it works! It's a creamy, fizzy beverage with a little hit of caffeine, and it's a fun non-boozy brunch treat—though you can add a shot of booze, if you like, and we won't judge you!

Ice cubes

½ cup (120 ml) whole milk

½ cup (120 ml) Pepsi

Liquor of your choice (optional)

Fill a pint glass with ice. Add milk to the halfway mark, then fill it the rest of the way with Pepsi. Add a shot of booze (vodka, rum, brandy, bourbon, and Kahlúa all work), if the mood strikes you.

Serves 1

Hair of the Dog Michelada

A michelada once saved Allison from one of the worst hangovers of her life: "It was Mother's Day 2012. Despite the brain-shattering headache and constant nausea racking my body, there was no way I was going to flake on my beloved mom. I looked at the brunch menu at Empellón Cocina (a fantastic Mexican restaurant here in NYC), desperately in need of a bit of hair of the dog that attacked me, and thought a michelada would be the gentlest option. It saved the day, restored me to being the doting daughter I aspire to be, and allowed me to enjoy some killer tacos."

This recipe is quite different from the one on Empellón's menu, but it does the job, and it does it deliciously. The salty, umami-rich Worcestershire and soy sauces balance out the fiery kick of the hot sauce and the bright, bracing acidity of the fresh lime juice. Sip it on ice and keep adding beer; by the time you've finished, you'll be able to remove your sunglasses.

Lime wedge

Kosher salt

Ice cubes

½ ounce Michelada Mix (opposite)

¾ ounce fresh lime juice

1 pint (480 ml) lager (we use Narragansett tallboy cans)

Moisten the rim of a pint glass with a lime wedge, then dip it in salt. Fill it with ice and add the Michelada Mix and lime juice. Top with the beer, and garnish with the lime wedge. Serve with a straw and the extra beer on the side for frequent top-offs.

Serves 1

MICHELADA MIX

Makes almost 1 cup (240 ml); enough for 15 micheladas

½ cup (120 ml) Worcestershire sauce
¼ cup (60 ml) Cholula hot sauce
2 tablespoons Tabasco hot sauce
1 tablespoon soy sauce

In a measuring cup, combine the Worcestershire, hot sauces, and soy sauce. Use immediately or store in an airtight container in the refrigerator for up to 6 months.

HEIRLOOM BLOODY MARYS

We thought it would be a fun challenge to take the best of summer's heirloom tomato crop and turn them into fresh, bright, bold riffs on the classic Bloody Mary cocktail. Inspired by the tomatoes' natural colors (green, red, and yellow), we use different spirits, herbs, and complementary ingredients to enhance them. The result is almost like a boozy gazpacho, full of texture and vibrant fresh vegetables. It's a pretty great way to feel healthy while consuming alcohol!

Bloody Mary Gets Fresh

This is a play on the most classic of Bloody Mary recipes, with a good dose of freshly grated horseradish, ripe red tomato, smoky chipotle, and celery salt. Enjoy it while the season lasts!

Combine the tomatoes and bell pepper in a blender along with the lemon juice, horseradish, olive brine, Worcestershire, chipotle puree, Tabasco, celery salt, black pepper, and salt. Puree until smooth.

Rim a pint glass with salt. Measure the vodka into the glass, fill it with ice, then pour in the tomato mixture. Stir well to incorporate and garnish with the celery stalk, lemon wedge, and a skewer of pickled veggies (see page 112 for recipes).

Serves 1

1 to 2 ripe red heirloom tomatoes, stemmed and chopped

1 red bell pepper, seeded and chopped

1 ounce fresh lemon juice

1 teaspoon freshly grated horseradish

1 teaspoon olive brine

½ teaspoon Worcestershire sauce

½ teaspoon chipotle puree (blend the contents of a can of chipotles in adobo)

¼ teaspoon Tabasco sauce

¼ teaspoon celery salt

¼ teaspoon freshly ground black pepper

¼ teaspoon kosher salt, plus more for the glass

2 ounces (60 ml) vodka (we like Reyka)

Ice cubes

Celery stalk, lemon wedge, and pickled veggies, for garnish

1.

2.

3.

Maria Verde

Green tomatoes and tomatillos show up at the farmers' market in late summer, and they complement each other perfectly. The jalapeño adds some fresh heat to the mixture, while the smoky mezcal lends depth and complexity. *Salud!*

In a blender, combine the tomato, tomatillos, jalapeño, lime juice, Tabasco, and salt and puree until smooth.

Rim a pint glass with salt. Measure the tequila and mezcal into the glass, fill it with ice, then pour in the tomato mixture. Stir well to incorporate and garnish with the pickled jalapeño, wedges of green tomato and pickled onion, and a lime wedge.

Serves 1

1 large green tomato, stemmed and chopped

1 or 2 tomatillos, husked and chopped

1 jalapeño pepper, seeded and chopped

1 ounce fresh lime juice

½ teaspoon Tabasco sauce

1 teaspoon kosher salt, plus more for the glass

1 ounce silver tequila (we like Espolón Blanco)

1 ounce Vida mezcal

Ice cubes

Pickled jalapeño, green tomato, pickled onion, and lime wedge, for garnish

Yellow Snapper

The botanical components of gin pair perfectly with fresh yellow tomatoes and tart ground cherries (aka cape gooseberries) in this bright summer cocktail, which is given a touch of smoke from some Islay malt Scotch.

In a blender, combine the tomato, ground cherries, bell pepper, lemon juice, hot sauce, and salt and puree until smooth.

Rim a pint glass with salt. Measure the gin and Scotch into the glass, fill it with ice, then pour in the tomato mixture. Stir well to incorporate, and garnish with the pickled onion, ground cherry, and lemon wedge.

Serves 1

1 large ripe yellow tomato, stemmed and chopped

6 to 8 ground cherries, husked and chopped

1 yellow bell pepper, seeded and chopped

1 ounce fresh lemon juice

½ teaspoon habanero hot sauce (our favorite is from local Brooklyn producer Queen Majesty)

1 teaspoon kosher salt, plus more for the glass

1½ ounces gin (we like the super-boozy Perry's Tot navy-strength gin from New York Distilling Company)

½ ounce Islay malt Scotch (Laphroaig 10 Year is a good choice)

Ice cubes

Pickled onion, ground cherry, and lemon wedge, for garnish

PICKLED VEGGIES

Ah, the pickle. One of the world's oldest ways of preserving food, and one of the best accompaniments to a Bloody Mary. Pickling not only makes veggies taste extremely delicious, but it also keeps fruits, veggies, and even fish from going bad for several months.

We use the "quick pickling" method for all of the pickles at our shop. This is the fastest way, and there's no fancy equipment needed—just a big pot and a heatproof container. You start by blanching your veggies, then pouring hot vinegar over the top. For some veggies, you don't even need to blanch them; the hot vinegar will cook them enough. It's fun to play around with the different types of vinegars and herbs used in each recipe to see how they affect the end flavor.

1. Cumin Carrots (page 117) \ 2. Gibson Onions (page 115)
\ 3. Spicy String Beans (page 116)

Pickled Beets & Onions

This is a two-in-one recipe: Not only do you get pickled beets when you make this, but also as the beets pickle in the vinegar, so do the red onions! You can snack on these on their own or use them in the Smoked Trout Benedict (page 82).

Preheat the oven to 400°F (205°C). Sterilize two 1-quart (1-L) glass jars with lids (see page 228).

Cut the beets in half and lay them on a baking sheet. Rub the beets with the olive oil, then cover the whole sheet in foil. Roast the beets for 30 to 40 minutes, or until you can easily pierce them with a fork. Set them aside to cool.

Once the beets have cooled, peel off and discard the skins, and cut them into 1-inch (2.5-cm) cubes. Divide the cubes evenly between the canning jars.

In a large pot, combine the vinegar, sugar, onions, salt, coriander, peppercorns, and star anise with 2 cups (480 ml) water and bring the mixture to a boil over high heat. Once the liquid starts to boil, take it off the heat and pour it evenly over the beets. If you're canning them, process them in a water bath. Otherwise, let them cool to room temperature, then refrigerate. The beets will keep for up to 2 months in the fridge.

Makes about 2 quarts (2 L)

4 medium beets (about 2 pounds / 910 g)

3 tablespoons olive oil

2 cups (480 ml) apple cider vinegar

1 cup (200 g) sugar

2 red onions, thinly sliced

1 tablespoon kosher salt

1 teaspoon whole coriander seeds

½ teaspoon whole black peppercorns

1 star anise pod

Gibson Onions

We kept this recipe incredibly basic with just coriander, peppercorns, and bay leaves as seasonings. This allows the sweet and peppery flavors of the onions to come through clearly. These would be an excellent accompaniment not only to Bloody Marys but also to a martini.

Sterilize two 1-quart (1-L) glass jars with lids (see page 228).

Place the onions in a medium saucepan and cover them with water. Bring them to a boil and cook for a few minutes, until tender. Strain the onions and divide them evenly between the canning jars.

In the same saucepan, bring the sugar, vinegar, coriander, peppercorns, bay leaves, and 1 cup (240 ml) water to a boil over high heat. Pour the liquid evenly over the onions. If you're canning them, process them in a water bath. Otherwise, let them cool to room temperature, then refrigerate. The onions will keep for up to 2 months in the fridge.

Makes about 2 quarts (2 L)

3 cups (330 g) pearl onions, peeled

1 cup (200 g) sugar

1 cup (240 ml) white vinegar

2 tablespoons coriander seeds

2 tablespoons whole black peppercorns

2 bay leaves

Spicy String Beans

These string beans are SPICY and continue to get spicier over time as they sit in the brine. You can easily control the amount of spice by simply cutting back on (or adding to!) the amount of red pepper flakes.

Sterilize two 1-quart (1-L) glass jars with lids (see page 228). Divide the string beans evenly between them.

In a medium saucepan, bring the vinegar, dill, garlic, sugar, peppercorns, red pepper flakes, coriander, bay leaves, salt, and 1¾ cups (420 ml) water to a boil over high heat. Pour the mixture evenly over the string beans. If you're canning them, process them in a water bath. Otherwise, let them cool to room temperature, then refrigerate. Let them sit for at least 24 hours before eating. The beans will keep for up to 2 months in the fridge.

Makes about 2 quarts (2 L)

2 pounds (910 g) string beans, cleaned and trimmed

2 cups (480 ml) apple cider vinegar

1 cup (50 g) fresh dill

12 whole garlic cloves, peeled

3 tablespoons sugar

2 tablespoons whole black peppercorns

2 tablespoons red pepper flakes

1 tablespoon coriander seeds

3 bay leaves

2 teaspoons kosher salt

Cumin Carrots

We go through more of these pickles in our shop than any of the others. The combination of the sweet carrots mixed with the potent cumin flavor leads to a very addicting snack.

Sterilize two 1-quart (1-L) glass jars with lids (see page 228). Divide the carrots evenly between them.

In a medium saucepan, bring the vinegar, dill, cumin, sugar, peppercorns, coriander, garlic, bay leaves, salt, and 1¾ cups (420 ml) water to a boil over high heat. Pour the mixture evenly over the carrots. If you're canning them, process them in a water bath. Otherwise, let them cool to room temperature, then refrigerate. Let them sit for at least 24 hours before eating. The carrots will keep for up to 2 months in the fridge.

Makes about 2 quarts (2 L)

2 pounds (910 g) carrots, peeled and cut into 1 by 3-inch (2.5 by 7.5-cm) sticks

1½ cups (360 ml) apple cider vinegar

½ cup (25 g) fresh dill

3 tablespoons cumin seeds

3 tablespoons sugar

2 tablespoons whole black peppercorns

1 tablespoon coriander seeds

12 whole garlic cloves, peeled

3 bay leaves

2 teaspoons kosher salt

Happy Hour

In New York, most of us live in **tiny apartments,** with no kitchen space and a roommate we don't want to confront until we've **thrown back** a few. This is why happy hour plays a very important role in our lives. It's a time to drink on the **cheap** (because we pay enormous sums for our tiny apartments) before heading out to dinner. It's also that time in the late afternoon between lunch and dinner, when all your **body and brain** need to **survive** is something sweet. For a bakery and bar, it is the **magic hour:** Candles are just getting placed on the tables, Sam Cooke is singing love songs in the background, and smells of freshly baked chocolate chip **cookies** envelop the bar while patrons clink their wineglasses. It's the time when the morning production bakers walk just a few feet from the kitchen to join the **after-work** crowd on the other side of the bar to chat about the day's **drama.** In this blissful hour, before **crowds descend** upon our bar, we've been able to get to know,

and even become **good friends** with, many of our customers.
We know it's been a bad day for Catherine when she
orders a **large**—not small—hot fudge sundae. We know to keep well
stocked with **High Life** in case Geoff shows up.
And there's no need to ask Frank what he wants when he comes
after church on Sunday afternoons—it's always a
slice of **pecan pie** with extra crust.

S'mores Bars

We got our start at an amazing outdoor food market here in Brooklyn called Smorgasburg, and we still pitch our tent there every weekend. Each day, about ten thousand people make their way through a sea of tents, filled with the aromas of everything from pupusas to lobster rolls to tempeh. Our tent might just smell the best, though, because the scent of toasting marshmallow is basically the best thing ever. (Why hasn't anyone bottled this as perfume yet?) These bars are basically a square version of the s'mores pie in Allison's other cookbook, *First Prize Pies*. It's a great way to scale up the portions for a party or a crowd, and just as delicious!

3 recipes Graham Cracker Crust (page 36)

1 pound 5 ounces (595 g) milk chocolate

3 cups (720 ml) heavy cream

3 large eggs

1 teaspoon kosher salt

3 tablespoons unflavored powdered gelatin

6 cups (1.2 kg) sugar

2 cups (480 ml) light corn syrup (see Note, page 39)

1 tablespoon vanilla extract

Press the graham cracker crust mixture into the bottom of a 13 by 18-inch (33 by 46-cm) baking sheet, making it as even as possible and taking care to reach the edges. Refrigerate until ready to use.

Preheat the oven to 350°F (175°C).

Put the milk chocolate in a large heatproof bowl. In a medium pot, heat the cream over medium heat until scalded. Pour it over the chocolate. Let the chocolate and cream stand for about 1 minute, then whisk until smooth. Whisk in the eggs and salt until completely blended.

Remove the crust from the fridge and pour the chocolate mixture over the crust. Bake it for about 25 minutes, or until the chocolate has set. Remove it from the oven to a wire rack to cool while you prepare the marshmallow.

RECIPE CONTINUES

In the bowl of a stand mixer fitted with the whisk attachment, pour in 2 cups (480 ml) cold water and sprinkle the gelatin over the top.

In a large saucepan, whisk the sugar and corn syrup with 1 cup (240 ml) water. Bring them to a boil over high heat and cook until the mixture reaches the hard ball stage on a candy thermometer (260°F / 127°C). Remove the pan from the heat, turn the stand mixer on low, and slowly and gently pour the hot syrup into the gelatin (be careful!). Try to avoid the sides of the bowl. Gradually increase the speed as the mixture thickens, until it's at the highest speed possible. Let the mixer run for 5 to 10 minutes, until the mixture has tripled in volume and is white and fluffy. Reduce the speed to low, add the vanilla, and mix until incorporated.

Pour the marshmallow over the cooled chocolate filling. Spread it out gently with a spatula. Using a kitchen torch (we recommend the Iwatani butane torch) or under your broiler (keep a close eye to prevent burning), toast the marshmallow to your ideal level of toastiness. Allow the marshmallow to firm up a bit (about 20 minutes at room temperature), then slice the slab into squares. If the marshmallow tries to stick to your knife, wet the knife frequently with hot water between slices. Wrap leftovers in plastic wrap misted with a bit of cooking spray to prevent it from sticking to the marshmallow. Keep refrigerated for up to 1 week. It's best to retoast the marshmallow before serving.

Makes fifteen 3-inch (7.5-cm) bars

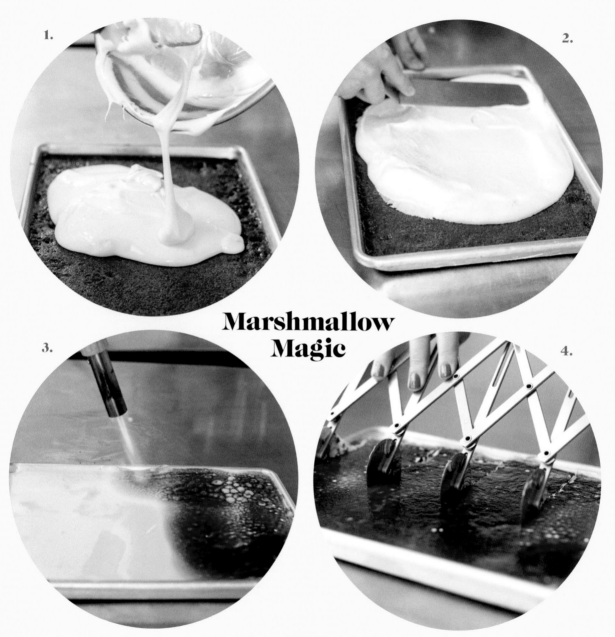

Marshmallow Magic

INSTRUCTIONS

1. Pour the marshmallow over the cooled chocolate filling.
2. Spread it out gently using a spatula. \ 3. Play with fire! Torch those babies until they're nice and toasty. \ 4. Allow the marshmallow to set for about 20 minutes, then slice into squares.

Kings County Corn Bowl Sundae

We signed up for the Kings County Corn Bowl competition in Brooklyn right after deciding to go into business together. It was an exciting moment for us because it was the first time we got to collaborate to create a dish. We fell into stride very naturally, bouncing ideas off each other, both of us bringing our quirky food ideologies to the table. We created a dish that neither one of us could have created alone. On the day of the event, our complementary styles paid off, and we won both the judges' and people's choice award for our Corn Bowl Sundae! It features Allison's mom's cornbread, doused in a good amount of spiced caramel sauce, layered with roasted corn ice cream and candied pistachios.

Place the cornbread at the bottom of a large sundae dish. Drench this in spiced caramel sauce, then top with three scoops of corn ice cream, more caramel sauce, and a sprinkling of candied pistachios. Serve immediately.

Serves 1

1 square Rhonda's Green Chile Cornbread (page 94), cut in half

½ cup (120 ml) Spicy Ginger Caramel Sauce (page 41)

3 scoops Roasted Corn Ice Cream (recipe follows)

¼ cup (30 g) Candied Pistachios (recipe follows)

Preheat the oven to 350°F (175°C).

Shuck the corn and cut off the kernels. Spread them out on a parchment- or foil-lined baking sheet and roast them for 15 to 20 minutes, or until they begin to turn golden brown in parts.

In a medium saucepan, heat 1½ cups (360 ml) of the milk with the cream over medium heat, until scalded. Add the roasted corn kernels and turn off the heat. Let the corn infuse into the liquid for 30 to 40 minutes. Strain out the corn (reserve the kernels for Rhonda's Green Chile Cornbread, page 94).

Whisk the sugar, corn syrup, and salt into the infused milk. Bring them to a boil over medium-high heat. Whisk together the remaining ½ cup (120 ml) of the milk and the cornstarch in a small bowl and add them to the infused milk. Stir constantly until the mixture thickens and coats the back of a spoon, about 2 minutes. In a small bowl, pour about ½ cup (120 ml) of the hot milk over the cream cheese and whisk until smooth. Add this back to the pot and whisk until smooth. Place the ice cream base in an airtight container and refrigerate for at least 8 hours before churning it into ice cream following the manufacturer's directions for your machine.

ROASTED CORN ICE CREAM

Makes 5 cups (1.2 L)

2 ears corn

2 cups (480 ml) whole milk

1¼ cups (300 ml) heavy cream

⅔ cup (135 g) sugar

2 tablespoons light corn syrup (see Note, page 39)

¼ teaspoon kosher salt

4 teaspoons cornstarch

3 tablespoons cream cheese

Preheat the oven to 350°F (175°C).

In a medium bowl, toss the pistachios, butter, sugar, oil, and salt together until the pistachios are totally coated. Spread them onto a parchment-lined rimmed baking sheet and place it in the oven. Roast for approximately 12 minutes, tossing every 3 to 4 minutes, until the pistachios are fragrant. Allow them to cool, then store them in an airtight container at room temperature for up to 1 month.

CANDIED PISTACHIOS

Makes 2½ cups (540 g)

2 cups (260 g) shelled pistachios, roughly chopped

1 cup (2 sticks / 225 g) unsalted butter, melted

¼ cup (55 g) firmly packed dark brown sugar

¼ cup (60 ml) canola oil

1¼ teaspoons kosher salt

Negroni Pie

We developed this recipe for our friends at Ward III, a beautiful cocktail bar in the Tribeca area of Manhattan. They were starting up a weekly industry night event geared toward bartenders and specifically wanted to serve slices of Negroni pie. More than game to try to turn one of our favorite cocktails into a dessert, we experimented with a few iterations before we landed on this winner. It's got all the components of the cocktail in the same ratios: equal parts Campari, gin, and sweet vermouth in a creamy custard, bolstered by our savory all-butter crust, and topped with an ethereal dollop of orange-zested whipped cream. Bitter, sweet, salty, and rich—it hits every spot.

Make the crust: In a small bowl, stir together the milk and vinegar, then refrigerate until ready to use.

On a clean flat surface or in a large shallow bowl, toss together the flour, sugar, and salt. Using a pastry blender, bench knife, or fork, cut the butter into the flour mixture until it is broken down into small, lentil-size pieces. Slowly drizzle in the milk mixture and toss with a fork to distribute it; be careful not to overwork the dough. Shape it into a disk, wrap it well in plastic, and refrigerate it for at least 1 hour.

RECIPE CONTINUES

For the crust:

- ⅓ cup (75 ml) whole milk
- 1 teaspoon apple cider vinegar
- 1⅓ cups (165 g) unbleached all-purpose flour, plus extra for rolling
- 1 tablespoon sugar
- ¾ teaspoon kosher salt
- ½ cup (1 stick / 115 g) cold unsalted European-style butter, cut into ½-inch (12-mm) cubes

For the filling:

- 1 (14-ounce / 396-g) can sweetened condensed milk
- 4 large egg yolks
- 2 ounces (60 ml) Campari
- 2 ounces (60 ml) dry gin
- 2 ounces (60 ml) sweet vermouth
- ¼ teaspoon kosher salt
- 1 or 2 drops red food coloring (optional)

For the topping:

- 1½ cups (360 ml) heavy cream
- 2 tablespoons sugar
- Zest of ½ orange

Preheat the oven to 425°F (220°C). Remove the dough from the fridge and allow it to warm up at room temperature for about 5 minutes. Gently manipulate the dough with your hands to make it pliable, then generously flour a clean cutting board or counter. Flour the dough and your rolling pin, and roll the dough out to 11 inches (28 cm) in diameter.

Transfer it to a 9-inch (23-cm) pie pan, trim the overhang to about 1 inch (2.5 cm), tuck the overhang under, and crimp it decoratively. Line the dough with foil. Fill the foil with dried beans or pie weights and blind-bake it for 20 minutes, rotating it once halfway through, until lightly golden around the edges and set on the bottom. Remove the crust from the oven; lower the heat to 350°F (175°C). Remove the foil and pie weights and allow the crust to cool completely while making the filling.

Make the filling: In a mixing bowl, whisk together the sweetened condensed milk, egg yolks, liquors, salt, and food coloring, if using. Pour the mixture into the blind-baked pie shell and bake until it is just barely set, 15 to 20 minutes. Remove it from the oven and let it cool completely before topping.

Make the topping: In a stand mixer fitted with the whisk attachment, whip the heavy cream and sugar together until soft peaks form. Top the pie with the whipped cream and sprinkle it with the orange zest. Leftovers can be refrigerated, loosely covered, and will keep for up to 3 days.

Makes one 10-inch (25-cm) pie; serves 8 to 10

Watchamacallthat Pie

This pie was inspired by both Allison's Trifecta Pie from *First Prize Pies* and by Keavy's deep love for the Whatchamacallit candy bar. When Keavy was a kid, she would take daily trips to the small local bait shop/candy store, and it was always a toss-up between a Snickers or a Whatchamacallit, though the Whatchamacallit almost always won out in the end. The combination of Rice Krispies, caramel, peanut butter, and chocolate creates the best textural experience you can ask for in a dessert. This pie should be eaten on a gloomy day, with a few close friends, a romcom, and a large bottle of wine.

Make the crust: In a medium saucepan, melt the butter over medium heat. Stir in the mini marshmallows and turn down the heat to medium-low, stirring constantly, until the marshmallows are melted. Add the Rice Krispies all at once and stir together until the marshmallow fully coats all the Rice Krispies. Dump this mixture into a 10-inch (25-cm) pie pan. In order to actually form this into a crust, you need your hands to be greasy. Take a tablespoon or two of butter and rub the palms of your hands with it. Then pat and press the Rice Krispie mixture into the pie pan to form an even, ½-inch- (12-mm-) thick pie crust.

Place in the refrigerator.

Make the caramel: In a small saucepan, combine the sugar, butter, and ¼ cup (60 ml) water. Bring them to a boil over medium-high heat. Continue boiling until the sugar caramelizes and turns a hazelnut color. Remove the pan from the heat and carefully whisk

RECIPE CONTINUES

For the Rice Krispie treat crust:

3 tablespoons unsalted butter, plus extra for shaping

3 cups (150 g) mini marshmallows

5 cups (125 g) Rice Krispies cereal

For the caramel:

½ cup (100 g) sugar

1 tablespoon unsalted butter

⅓ cup (75 ml) heavy cream

¼ teaspoon kosher salt

For the peanut butter layer:

½ cup (120 ml) heavy cream

⅓ cup (75 ml) smooth peanut butter, at room temperature

⅓ cup (40 g) confectioners' sugar

3 ounces (85 g) cream cheese, at room temperature

¾ teaspoon kosher salt

For the topping:

½ cup (85 g) chopped bittersweet chocolate

¼ cup (60 ml) heavy cream

in the heavy cream and salt. Immediately pour this mixture into your Rice Krispie crust. Pick up the pie tin and carefully rotate it, helping to spread the caramel around the upper sides of the crust. Immediately put it back into the fridge.

Make the peanut butter layer: In a small bowl, combine the cream, peanut butter, confectioners' sugar, cream cheese, and salt and mix them together with a spatula or wooden spoon. When the mixture starts to come together, switch to a whisk and whisk the mixture until totally smooth. Pour this into the Rice Krispie crust, smoothing it out into a thin layer, then place it back in the fridge.

Make the topping: Place the chocolate in a heatproof bowl. In a small saucepan, bring the heavy cream to a boil and pour it over the chocolate. Let it sit for 30 seconds, then whisk the mixture together until smooth.

Pour the chocolate mixture over the peanut butter layer and, very carefully with a spatula, spread it out to the sides of the crust, trying not to mix it with the peanut butter.

Place the whole pie back in the fridge and let it chill for at least 30 minutes before serving. The pie will keep, wrapped in plastic, for up to 1 week in the fridge, or in the freezer for up to 2 months.

Makes one 10-inch (25-cm) pie; serves 8 to 10

Twin Peaks Special

Allison's a freak for the old TV series *Twin Peaks*. She loves everything about it and wishes she could teleport herself to the Double R Diner to hang out with Agent Dale Cooper over a damn fine cup of coffee. Pie and coffee are a classic pairing for a reason, and because we like to introduce booze as an option whenever possible, we've got a bit of it in each component of this pairing. We think Dale would be okay with it!

RECIPE CONTINUES

Preheat the oven to 425°F (220°C). Allow the dough to rest for about 5 minutes after taking it out of the fridge, then divide it in half. Lightly flour a work surface and roll half of the dough into a circle about 11 inches (28 cm) in diameter. Transfer it to a 10-inch (25-cm) pie pan and refrigerate.

In a large bowl, toss together the cherries, liqueur (if using), and vanilla. In a small bowl, whisk together the brown sugar, cornstarch, and salt.

Roll out the second round of dough to 12 inches (30.5-cm) and cut it into 6 large lattice strips, about 2 inches (5 cm) wide. Add the sugar mixture to the cherries, toss to coat them, and pour that into the crust-lined pie pan.

Arrange the lattice strips over the top. Lay one strip across the center of your filling. Lay another strip across the middle, perpendicular to the first strip. Then lay two strips perpendicular to that strip, on either side. Peel back one side of the bottom-most strip, lay a strip down perpendicular to that one, and cover it. Repeat on the other side. Tuck any overhang under the bottom crust and crimp it decoratively.

In a small bowl, whisk together the egg with the water or milk. Brush the crust with the egg wash and sprinkle it with raw sugar. Put it on a baking sheet and bake for 20 minutes, rotating the pie once halfway through, then lower the heat to 350°F (175°C). Bake the pie for another 30 to 40 minutes, until the crust is golden brown and the filling bubbling up through the lattice is thick and glossy. Remove the pie to a wire rack to cool before serving. Wrap leftovers in plastic and refrigerate for up to 5 days.

CHERRY PIE

Makes one 10-inch (25-cm) pie; serves 8 to 10

1 recipe All-Butter Pie Crust (page 34)

Flour, for dusting

2 pounds (910 g) sour cherries, pitted

2 tablespoons Cherry Heering liqueur (optional)

1 teaspoon vanilla extract

1 cup (220 g) firmly packed dark brown sugar

¼ cup (30 g) cornstarch

¼ teaspoon kosher salt

1 large egg

¼ cup (60 ml) water or milk

Raw sugar, for sprinkling

A DAMN FINE CUP OF COFFEE

We're not going to tell you how to brew a cup of coffee, other than to say: Use good, fresh beans and brew it strong. If you want a little extra kick in the pants (it gets cold in Twin Peaks, you know), add a shot of Scotch—the smokiness goes great with the sweet, tart cherries in the pie!

BOOZY FLOATS

1.

2.

BOOZY FLOATS

One of our favorite pastimes at Butter & Scotch is taking classic soda-fountain treats and making them just a bit more grown-up. We thought it would be fun to riff on ice cream floats, but using beer and booze instead of the traditional soda. The result is decidedly more adult, with a hefty dose of bitterness to temper the sweetness of the ice cream, while still keeping the fizzy fun of the beautiful original.

3.

4.

PRETTY IN PINK

Serves 1

This lovely rose-colored float combines rosé wine, Aperol
(a bright, citrusy liqueur), a splash of seltzer, and a scoop of strawberry ice
cream. It's refreshing, delicious, and not too sweet—the flavor of the
strawberry really shines through.

Measure the rosé and Aperol into a pint or soda glass.
Add the ice cream, then top with seltzer. Serve
with a spoon and a straw.

3 ounces (90 ml) dry rosé wine
1 ounce Aperol liqueur
1 scoop strawberry ice cream
Seltzer

ROOT & BEER FLOAT

Serves 1

1 ounce ROOT liqueur

1 ounce Simplest Simple Syrup (page 47)

1 scoop vanilla ice cream

Stout beer (we use Brooklyn Brewery's Black Chocolate Stout)

We were asked to devise a boozy float for the Amy Atlas blog *Sweet Designs,* and it led to this delicious creation! Inspired by the classic root beer float, we decided to make it boozy by using real beer and ROOT liqueur, which is one of our favorite cocktail ingredients. Unlike cloying root beer schnapps, you really taste all of the herbs and spices that go into good root beer in this liqueur, and there's an edge of bitterness as well.

Measure the liqueur and simple syrup into a pint or soda glass. Add the ice cream, then top with the stout. Serve with a spoon and straw.

APPLE PIE FLOAT

Serves 1

We have hard cider on tap at the bar, and it's one of
Allison's favorite post-work-shift drinks. The quality
of craft ciders keeps growing, and you can get an incredible range of
options at any good beer store and even in a lot of supermarkets
these days. We wanted to riff on the flavors of apple pie à la mode, but in cool,
creamy float form. This is what we landed on, and it is delicious.

Measure the amaro into a pint or soda glass,
add the ice cream, and top with the cider. Serve
with a spoon and straw.

1 ounce Brovo amaro
(see Note)

1 scoop vanilla ice cream

Hard cider
(we use Doc's Draft cider)

NOTE: If you can't find the
delicious, small-batch amaro
that we use, a spiced rum is a
great alternative.

BITTERSWEET

Serves 1

1 ounce Zucca amaro
(see Note)

1 scoop coffee ice cream

IPA (we use Goose Island IPA)

NOTE: If you have another amaro you love, give it a try instead! This recipe is pretty adaptable to a range of amari.

The most boldly bitter of our beer floats, this marries hop-heavy IPA with Zucca (a rhubarb amaro), and coffee ice cream for another layer of bitter-sweetness. If you like the kick of an IPA, give this a try for a fun, summery alternative to plain old beer.

Measure the amaro into a pint or soda glass, add the ice cream, and top with the beer. Serve with a spoon and straw.

HOTTIES

Winters in New York are rough. That first, pristine layer of fresh snowfall very quickly mixes with truck exhaust and unspeakable dirt to form quicksand-like pits of slush that will happily devour your cute little rainboot if you unwittingly step too deep. Days (let's be honest, *months*) like this will leave you in need of something hot and alcoholic to recover and remember why on earth you live here. That's where our Hotties come in!

1.

2.

3.

4.

5.

Hot Buttered Scotch

We first opened up shop in the dead of winter, and we knew we'd need at least one great mug of hot booze on offer. Allison created this recipe as part of a special reward for our Kickstarter backers (without whose help we'd never have opened our doors!). We wanted something with both butter and Scotch (obvs!) and thought a riff on the classic hot buttered rum just might work. It really does. There's a bit of peaty smoke from the Islay malt Scotch, which helps balance out the sweet brown sugar, rich butter, and citrus and spice of allspice dram and orange zest. It'll warm you up!

In a small bowl, whip the cream, sugar, and orange zest until soft peaks form. Set aside.

In a mixing bowl, beat together the brown sugar, butter, and salt until fluffy. Whisk in the boiling water, allspice, and whiskies until fully blended. Pour the mixture into two warm mugs, top with dollops of whipped cream and a little more orange zest, and serve hot.

Serves 2

¼ cup (60 ml) heavy cream

1 tablespoon sugar

Zest of ½ orange, plus more for garnish

¼ cup (55 g) firmly packed dark brown sugar

¼ cup (½ stick / 55 g) unsalted butter, at room temperature

½ teaspoon kosher salt

1 cup (240 ml) boiling water

1 teaspoon allspice dram (or a pinch of powdered allspice)

3 ounces (90 ml) smooth blended Scotch whisky (such as Monkey Shoulder)

1 ounce Islay malt Scotch whisky (such as Laphroaig)

Peppermint Patty

Once fall hits New York and all of Brooklyn starts donning tights and leather jackets, we begin to get requests for boozy hot chocolate. Instead of using an overly sweet instant hot cocoa mix, we use ample amounts of our Hot Fudge mixed with steamed local milk. And to give this its boozy kick and a nice minty flavor, we add in a few ounces Brancamenta.

In a large liquid measuring cup, combine the Brancamenta and hot fudge. Add the steamed milk and whisk them together. Divide the mixture between two mugs and top them with the whipped cream and a dusting of cocoa powder.

Serves 2

3 ounces (90 ml) Brancamenta

¼ cup (60 ml) Hot Fudge (page 39), warmed

1 cup (240 ml) whole milk, steamed

½ cup (120 ml) Whipped Cream (page 45)

Unsweetened cocoa powder, for garnish

Porto Quente

We came up with this recipe in the dead of winter, when we really needed something with vitamin C to help stave off any risk of scurvy. This is an ideal recipe for a winter party, as you can pour it all in a slow-cooker and let your guests serve themselves!

Peel the rinds from the oranges and grapefruit and muddle them with the brown sugar in a large bowl. Allow this to sit for at least 30 minutes, to release the oils in the rinds.

In a large pot, boil 2 cups (480 ml) water. Add the muddled rinds, then the star anise, cinnamon, cloves, and mace, if using. Juice the oranges and grapefruit and add the juice to the pot. Simmer over medium heat for 10 minutes. Strain out the solids, turn the heat down to very low (or transfer the liquid to a slow cooker set on warm). Add the port and both types of bitters. Make sure the mixture stays hot, but not boiling, and serve it in mugs.

**Makes enough for a party!
(approximately 10 servings)**

2 oranges

1 grapefruit

¼ cup (55 g) firmly packed dark brown sugar

1 star anise pod

1 cinnamon stick

4 whole cloves

1 whole mace (optional)

1 (750-ml) bottle ruby port

5 dashes Angostura bitters

5 dashes Regan's orange bitters (optional)

Rhonda's Ruby Toddy

Allison's mom, Rhonda, is a former bartender and has a pretty liberal pour with the spirits. Whenever Allison and her brother, Corwin, would get sick as kids, rather than resorting to a pharmacy run for NyQuil, their mom would whip up her homemade version: the hot toddy. Allison grew to know (and like) the taste of bourbon from a pretty young age, and for that she's thankful! Rhonda's version is classic, except for one great addition: hibiscus. It gives a gorgeous ruby hue to the drink, as well as a floral, citrusy brightness.

2 ounces (60 ml) good bourbon

¾ ounce Hibiscus-Honey Simple Syrup (recipe follows)

¼ ounce fresh lemon juice

Boiling water

Lemon wedge, for garnish

Serves 1

Measure the bourbon, hibiscus syrup, and lemon juice into a big mug. Fill the mug with boiling water, stir, and let it sit until it's cool enough to drink. Garnish with a lemon wedge. Drink it, and feel better!

HIBISCUS-HONEY SIMPLE SYRUP

Makes 1½ cups (360 ml)

1 cup (240 ml) honey
¼ cup (8 g) dried hibiscus flowers

In a small saucepan, stir the honey, hibiscus, and ½ cup (120 ml) water over medium heat until the honey has dissolved. Pour the mixture into an airtight container and allow it to infuse overnight in the fridge. Strain out and discard the hibiscus flowers. The syrup will keep for up to 1 month in the refrigerator.

Bitter Medicine

Sometimes a touch of something bitter is just what you need after a meal of sweets. Cynar is a delicious and affordable amaro (made with artichoke!), with a great balance of bitter and sweet. The burnt-sugar undertones in the molasses and bitter edge of the coffee complement it perfectly.

In a small bowl, whip the cream and sugar until soft peaks form. Set aside.

Measure the amaro and molasses into a mug, and top with the coffee. Stir to dissolve the molasses, top with the whipped cream, and serve.

2 tablespoons heavy cream

1 teaspoon sugar

2 ounces (60 ml) Cynar amaro

1 teaspoon molasses

5 ounces (150 ml) hot brewed coffee

Serves 1

Literally & Figuratively

This beverage is literally hot, in that it is served at a high temperature, and it is figuratively hot, in that it's a bit spicy! Thus concludes our grammar lesson for the day. This is made with Ancho Reyes, a gorgeous ancho chile liqueur that is great in any number of cocktails (including the Grilled Pineapple on page 153). If you want something to warm you from your head down to your toes, this is your guy.

Measure the tequila, ancho liqueur, lime juice, and agave into a mug. Top with boiling water and stir well to dissolve. Garnish with a lime wheel tossed in red pepper flakes.

1 ounce Espolón Blanco tequila or silver tequila of your choice

1 ounce Ancho Reyes liqueur

½ ounce fresh lime juice

½ ounce agave syrup

Boiling water

1 lime wheel

1 teaspoon red pepper flakes

Serves 1

Grilled Pineapple

This recipe by Jen Marshall (our friend, partner, and opening beverage director) was given an added stroke of brilliance by Mike Nicolini, one of our former bartenders. Inspired by the smoky, tropical flavors of the pineapple and mezcal, he suggested a very unorthodox garnish: HAM! We gave it a go, and it really takes this one over the top. If you like Hawaiian pizza, you'll understand.

Fill a cocktail shaker with ice and add the tequila, pineapple juice, mezcal, ancho liqueur, lemon juice, and simple syrup. Give it a hard shake, then double-strain the liquid into a chilled coupe and garnish it with a skewer of seared ham cubes.

Serves 1

Ice cubes

1 ounce silver tequila (we use Espolón Blanco)

1 ounce pineapple juice

½ ounce mezcal (we use Del Maguey's Vida)

½ ounce Ancho Reyes liqueur

½ ounce fresh lemon juice

½ ounce Simplest Simple Syrup (page 47)

Thick-cut Berkshire ham, seared and cut into cubes, for garnish

Menta
Make a Julep

For some silly reason, we were a bit stumped when trying to come up with a whiskey cocktail for our summer menu last year. Finally, Allison looked up at the back bar shelves and her eyes traveled over a bottle of Brancamenta. In case you're unfamiliar, it's a bitter, very minty amaro—quite different from the crème de menthe you might have seen in your grandparents' liquor cabinet. She played around and found that it makes a great, muddle-free mint julep: a super-boozy, slushy, summer sipper.

Measure the rye and simple syrup into a rocks glass. Fill the glass to overflowing with crushed ice, then top it with the Brancamenta. Garnish with a mint sprig.

Serves 1

2 ounces (60 ml) rye whiskey (we use Old Overholt)

1 ounce Molasses Simple Syrup (page 49)

Crushed ice (see page 229)

¼ ounce Brancamenta

Fresh mint sprig, for garnish

Rhubarb Sour

We loooooove rhubarb. It's great in pie, as we all know, but we wanted to add its bright, fresh flavor to a cocktail without losing its subtle, aromatic qualities. This is a great way to use one of our favorite fleeting spring ingredients.

To make rhubarb juice, puree the chopped rhubarb in a blender (add as little water as possible to get a puree, 1 tablespoon at a time). Strain it through a sieve, refrigerate, and use the juice within 2 days. Reserve the solids to make the rhubarb simple syrup (opposite page).

In a cocktail shaker, combine the rye, 1 ounce of the rhubarb juice, the simple syrup, and lemon juice with ice, and shake until chilled. Double-strain the drink into a chilled cocktail glass, and serve.

Serves 1

2 stalks rhubarb, chopped into small pieces

2 ounces (60 ml) rye whiskey (we use Old Overholt)

¾ ounce Rhubarb Simple Syrup (recipe follows)

½ ounce fresh lemon juice

Ice cubes

RHUBARB SIMPLE SYRUP

Makes 1 pint (480 ml)

1 cup (200 g) sugar
Rhubarb solids (reserved from Rhubarb Sour, opposite)

In a small saucepan, combine the sugar, rhubarb solids, and 1 cup (240 ml) water. Stir over medium heat until the sugar has dissolved, then remove from the heat and allow it to stand for at least 1 hour, or up to overnight, to infuse the syrup. Strain out and discard the rhubarb solids and store the syrup in the refrigerator for up to 1 month.

Lady Boss Daiquiri

We created this drink for Lady Boss, a women-owned business seminar we took part in. It's a riff on a daiquiri with the addition of passion fruit and a molasses simple syrup, which gives it some depth. It's strong and assertive, like a lady boss needs to be!

Fill a cocktail shaker with ice. Measure the rum, lime juice, simple syrup, passion fruit, and molasses simple syrup into it and shake hard until well chilled. Double strain the liquid into a chilled cocktail glass and top with the lime wheel.

Ice cubes

1½ ounces light rum (we use Owney's)

½ ounce fresh lime juice

½ ounce Simplest Simple Syrup (page 47)

¼ ounce passion fruit puree (see Note, page 92)

¼ ounce Molasses Simple Syrup (page 49)

Lime wheel, for garnish

Serves
1

Union Street Collins

Our opening beverage director, Jen Marshall, created this cocktail for our debut menu. It's named after the street directly to our left in Crown Heights and was inspired by the large West Indian population in the neighborhood.

    With its hot-pink color from the hibiscus syrup and its bright lemon notes, this drink reminds me of an adult version of pink lemonade. It goes down a little too easy and is perfect for an afternoon cocktail on a hot summer's day.

Fill a cocktail shaker with ice. Measure the vodka, lemon juice, and syrup into it and shake well until chilled. Strain the liquid into a Collins glass over 4 ice cubes and top with seltzer, the bitters, and the lemon wheel.

Serves 1

Ice cubes

1½ ounces vodka (we use Reyka)

1 ounce fresh lemon juice

1 ounce Hibiscus-Clove Syrup (page 49)

Seltzer

3 dashes Fee's Aromatic Bitters

Lemon wheel, for garnish

Night

At Butter & Scotch, we get **ready for the rush**
a bit later than most food establishments. While everyone's out
eating their savory stuff, we have a quiet few who know the value
of dessert for dinner (we love you guys!). After dinner is when we get really
busy—everyone's ready for a change of scenery, a well-crafted cocktail, and
sugar. We are more than happy to oblige on all counts;
nighttime is the right time for a bit more of everything. The
music goes up, the desserts get even more **indulgent**, and
the drinks get maybe just a *smidge* stronger.

FUN PAIRINGS

When writing the menu for Butter & Scotch, we didn't want to focus too much on pairings. We wanted the ordering process to be more natural and fun than that. Our bartenders are fully trained to help a guest pair his or her drink with one of our desserts, but if you exclusively want to drink Chardonnay with your chocolate cake, who are we to stop you? Following are a few of the pairings that we do have on our menu.

The Mary Ellen

A Dry Vodka Martini and a Classic Hot Fudge Sundae

Keavy's grandmother Mary Ellen was a wonderful woman with a life straight out of *Mad Men*. She lounged by the pool with a martini and blonde bouffant in the morning, bet on the ponies from the boxes in the afternoon, and took drags off cigars while chanting Irish tunes in the evenings. When Keavy was old enough to take her out to dinner, Mary Ellen would always order a small cup of clam chowder but never eat it. When the server asked her if she was happy with her meal, she would coyly explain she just wasn't hungry, but would LOVE a hot fudge sundae and a dry vodka martini . . . three olives, please.

CLASSIC HOT FUDGE SUNDAE

Serves 1

Put a third of the hot fudge at the bottom of a sundae glass. Top with one scoop of the ice cream. Repeat this process two more times. Top with the whipped cream, toasted almonds, and cherry.

1 cup (240 ml) Hot Fudge (page 39)

3 scoops vanilla ice cream

¼ cup (60 ml) Whipped Cream (page 45)

1 tablespoon slivered almonds, toasted

1 maraschino cherry (we use Fabbri)

DRY VODKA
MARTINI

Serves 1

3 ounces (90 ml) vodka
   (make it a good one!)
¼ ounce dry vermouth
Ice cubes
3 olives

In a mixing glass, stir the
vodka and vermouth with
ice until chilled. Strain
them into a chilled martini
glass and garnish with the
olives.

Make It Sparkle

A Slice of Birthday Cake & a Glass of Bubbly

The recipe for our birthday cake was born from one of the happiest accidents we've had at Butter & Scotch.

Hours before the opening party for our friends and family, our baker Lindsey baked a cake for us to serve at the celebration. But when she took the layers out of the oven, they all sank! Without time to bake more, we just lopped off the tops of each cake round and frosted them anyway. It turned out she had inadvertently omitted almost half of the flour that the original recipe called for, and in doing so had created the best vanilla cake we've ever tasted. We immediately adjusted the recipe to the "mistake" version and still bake it this way at the shop. It's basically the dictionary definition of a happy accident!

This pairing was inspired by Ashley and Kristen, two regulars who have a monthly friend date to eat cake and drink bubbly at the bar. We serve our version with a crisp, dry cava, but any dry sparkling wine (look for "brut" or "extra brut" on the label if you're not sure) will be a great foil to the sweet, creamy richness of this cake. And if you feel like a splurge, real-deal Champagne would not be unwelcome here!

BIRTHDAY CAKE

Makes one 9-inch (23-cm) 3-layer cake; serves 12 to 20

Preheat the oven to 350°F (175°C). Butter three 9-inch (23-cm) round cake pans. Dust with a few tablespoons of flour, then tap out the excess.

Chop the butter into small, pea-size pieces and return them to the refrigerator. Bring the milk to room temperature by zapping it in the microwave for 30 seconds, then add the vanilla and set it aside.

In the bowl of a stand mixer fitted with the paddle attachment, combine the flour, 2½ cups (500 g) of the sugar, the baking powder, and salt. Mix on low for 30 seconds. Add the cold butter to the flour mixture and bring the speed up to medium. Mix until the butter breaks down and the flour mixture is the texture of wet sand. Bring the speed back down to low and add the milk mixture. Transfer the mixture into a large bowl and set aside.

Fully clean and dry out the bowl of the mixer, swap out the paddle for the whisk attachment, and add the egg whites and remaining 1½ cups (300 g) sugar to the bowl. Whisk on high until the mixture forms soft peaks. Gently fold the meringue into the flour and milk mixture until fully incorporated.

Divide the batter equally between the prepared pans and bake them for 30 to 40 minutes, rotating halfway through, until they are golden brown and a cake tester comes out clean.

Transfer the pans to a wire rack for 10 minutes before turning the cakes out of the pans to cool completely. Using a serrated knife, trim the tops off the cakes to make them level and frost and stack the three layers. Decorate the side with rainbow sprinkles and the top with frosting rosettes. Serve a slice with a glass of bubbly.

Store at room temperature in a cake dome or large plastic Tupperware for up to 3 days.

2 cups (4 sticks / 455 g) cold unsalted butter, plus more for the pans

4 cups (500 g) unbleached all-purpose flour, plus more for pans

2¾ cups (660 ml) whole milk

2 tablespoons vanilla extract

4 cups (800 g) sugar

¼ cup (50 g) baking powder

2 teaspoons kosher salt

12 large egg whites

2 recipes Keavy's Favorite Vanilla Frosting (page 28)

Rainbow sprinkles, for garnish

Milk & a Cookie

White Russian & a Salted Chocolate Chip Cookie

WHITE RUSSIAN

Serves 1

Measure the vodka and Kahlúa into a rocks glass. Fill it with ice, then top with the milk. Stir and enjoy!

2 ounces (60 ml) vodka (we use Reyka)

1 ounce Kahlúa liqueur

Ice cubes

2 ounces (60 ml) whole milk

SALTED CHOCOLATE CHIP COOKIES

Makes 2 dozen

For Keavy, a chocolate chip cookie is one of the most perfect desserts ever created, and she eats one, without guilt, every single day.

We can't remember how many variations we created before landing on this one, but it must have been at least two dozen. Every day we would have a different cookie at the shop, and every day we would notice something that needed changing. After about a month of rotating cookies (and very patient customers), we nailed it: crunchy on the outside, chewy on the inside, a hefty amount of brown butter and dark chocolate, and a nice crunch of salt on top.

The one downside is that this amazing cookie requires patience: You must, *must* let the dough chill overnight. It truly is the difference between an average cookie and an incredible one. We think you'll find it's worth the wait!

In a small saucepan over medium-high heat, bring the butter to a boil. You're turning this into brown butter, or *beurre noisette*: when the butter starts to foam, and you smell a nutty aroma, immediately remove it from the heat. Be careful, as brown butter can quickly turn to burnt butter if you let it go too far. Allow it to cool slightly, and then whisk in ½ cup (120 ml) of the water.

In a large bowl, whisk together both sugars, then whisk in the brown butter mixture. In a medium bowl, whisk together the remaining ⅓ cup (75 ml) water, the egg yolks, the oil, and the vanilla until combined. Whisk the egg mixture into the butter-and-sugar mixture until combined.

In a separate medium bowl, stir together the flour, baking soda, and salt. Stir the dry ingredients into the wet ingredients in two additions until fully incorporated. Fold in the chocolate chips.

Cover the bowl with plastic wrap and refrigerate overnight (this allows the dough to fully hydrate, and prevents the cookies from spreading too much during baking).

Preheat the oven to 350°F (175°C).

With a ½-cup (120-ml) ice cream scoop, scoop the dough onto two parchment-lined baking sheets. (If you want to have some cookies for another time, or don't want to bake a full batch, cover the extra scooped dough with plastic wrap and freeze for up to 1 month.)

Gently press down on each cookie with the palm of your hand to flatten it a bit. Sprinkle a pinch of *fleur du sel* on each cookie. Bake for 10 minutes, rotating the baking sheets once halfway through, until the cookies are golden around the edges and light in the center. Allow to cool before serving. Store in an airtight container at room temperature for up to 2 days.

1½ cups (3 sticks / 340 g) unsalted butter

½ cup plus ⅓ cup (195 ml) cold water

1⅔ cups (335 g) granulated sugar

1⅔ cups (365 g) dark brown sugar

8 large egg yolks

⅓ cup (75 ml) canola oil

2 tablespoons vanilla extract

1 pound 10 ounces (approximately 6 cups / 750 g) unbleached all-purpose flour

2¾ teaspoons baking soda

1 tablespoon plus 1 teaspoon kosher salt

12 ounces (340 g) bittersweet chocolate chips

Fleur du sel (we use Maldon), for garnish

PB&J

Concord Gin Fizz & Peanut Butter Pie

If you haven't noticed by now, we enjoy taking the nostalgic flavors of our childhoods and transforming them into something just a bit more grown-up. Case in point: our version of a PB&J (that's peanutbutterandjelly, for those of you who grew up on the moon, or at least outside the United States!). Instead of a smooshy sandwich on Wonder Bread (oh man, that sounds good right now), we divvy up the ingredients, pairing a slice of peanut butter pie with a cool, tart, and refreshing Concord Gin Fizz cocktail. Not exactly like Mom used to make!

CONCORD GIN FIZZ

Serves 1

In a cocktail shaker, muddle the grapes until they've released a deep purple juice. Add the grape juice, gin, port, lemon juice, egg white, and sugar and shake vigorously, without ice, for 30 seconds (this helps to emulsify the egg white). Add ice and shake for 1 more minute. Double-strain the liquid into a chilled cocktail glass, top with a splash of seltzer, and garnish with the lemon twist. Serve.

5 Concord grapes

2 ounces (60 ml) Concord grape juice

1½ ounces gin

1 ounce tawny port

¼ ounce fresh lemon juice

1 large egg white

1 teaspoon superfine sugar

Ice cubes

Seltzer

1 lemon twist, for garnish

PEANUT BUTTER PIE

Makes one 9-inch (23-cm) pie

Preheat the oven to 350°F (175°C).

In a food processor, pulse the cookies with ¼ teaspoon of the salt until finely ground. Scrape the crumbs into a 9-inch (23-cm) pie pan. Stir in the melted butter, ½ tablespoon at a time, until the crumbs are the texture of wet sand; you may not need to use all of the butter. Using your fingers, press the crumbs evenly over the bottom and up the side of the pie pan. Freeze the crust for 15 minutes.

Bake the crust for about 10 minutes, until lightly golden. Let it cool on a rack.

In a medium bowl, combine the peanut butter with the cream cheese, ½ cup (65 g) of the confectioners' sugar, and the remaining ¼ teaspoon of the salt; mix until thoroughly blended. In another bowl, whip ¾ cup (180 ml) of the heavy cream until stiff. Whisk the whipped cream into the peanut butter mixture. Spread the peanut butter filling in the crust in an even layer. Refrigerate it until chilled, about 30 minutes.

In the same whipped-cream bowl, whip the remaining 1 cup (240 ml) heavy cream and 2 tablespoons confectioners' sugar with the vanilla until stiff. Spread the whipped cream over the pie. Sprinkle the pie with the chopped peanuts, cut it into slices, and serve. Wrap leftovers loosely in plastic and refrigerate for up to 5 days.

8 ounces (225 g) peanut butter sandwich cookies, such as Nutter Butter

½ teaspoon kosher salt

About ¼ cup (½ stick / 55 g) unsalted butter, melted

½ cup (120 ml) creamy peanut butter

4 ounces (115 g) cream cheese, at room temperature

½ cup plus 2 tablespoons (80 g) confectioners' sugar

1¾ cups (420 ml) heavy cream

1 teaspoon vanilla extract

¼ cup (35 g) salted roasted peanuts, coarsely chopped

Eggnog Pudding

Guys, Allison doesn't like eggnog. She really likes the idea of it, and she likes making it, but there's something about drinking a cup of eggy, creamy booze that just gives her the heebies, and we know she's not alone here. However, we've discovered that by taking the components of eggnog and turning them into desserts, we get to enjoy those great wintry flavors without having to force them down. So if you're with her on the whole eggnog-is-gross thing, try this pudding and be a Grinch no more!

In a medium pot, heat 4 cups (960 ml) of the milk with the vanilla pod and seeds over medium heat until steaming. In a medium bowl, whisk together the remaining ½ cup (120 ml) milk, the sugar, egg yolks, cornstarch, and salt. Once the milk in the pot is hot, ladle a few thin streams of it into the egg yolk mixture, whisking constantly, to temper the yolks. Then whisk the contents of the bowl into the pot of hot milk and continue to cook, whisking steadily, until the mixture boils and thickens to a pudding consistency. You should be able to see whisk marks in the surface of the pudding, and it should coat the back of a spoon.

Remove the pudding from the heat and whisk in the nutmeg, rum, and brandy. Push the hot pudding through a fine-mesh sieve to remove any lumps, spoon it into individual cups, then refrigerate it until cool (press plastic wrap or wax paper onto the top of the pudding to prevent a skin from forming). Serve the cold puddings topped with whipped cream and a fresh grating of nutmeg.

Serves 4 to 6

4½ cups (1 L) whole milk

1 vanilla bean, split and scraped

1 cup (200 g) sugar

5 large egg yolks, beaten

⅓ cup (45 g) cornstarch

¼ teaspoon kosher salt

¼ teaspoon freshly grated nutmeg, plus more for garnish

2 ounces (60 ml) amber rum

2 ounces (60 ml) brandy

Whipped Cream (page 45), for garnish

Pie (& Cake & Cookie) Shake

Allison's boyfriend, Jay, hails from Cedar Rapids, Iowa, and every time they go back to visit his family, she insists on a visit to Hamburg Inn in Iowa City. It's everything a diner should be: photos of staff and patrons on the walls, cozy wooden booths and a soda fountain–style counter, crazy-reasonable prices, and delicious, straightforward food. It's there that she first discovered the Pie Shake, a creation that ups the ante on dessert by combining two into one. It's just what it sounds like: a milkshake with a piece of pie blended in. We don't think we need to say anything more to convince you to try it. We've got 'em on the menu at all times at Butter & Scotch, and we like to mix it up with slices of cake and chocolate chip cookies sometimes, too!

In a blender, process the ice cream and milk together until smooth and milkshakey. Turn the blender off, plop in the pie/cake/cookie, and blend for another 5 to 10 seconds, until the pie has broken down somewhat but is still a bit chunky. Pour the shake into a pint glass and top it with whipped cream and a cherry, if using. Serve with a spoon and a straw!

4 scoops of ice cream (flavor of your choice)

¼ cup (60 ml) whole milk

1 slice of pie (or cake or a cookie)

Whipped cream (page 45), for garnish

A cherry on top (optional)

Serves 1

Cheese Puffs

When she was growing up, Keavy's family had two freezers in the house: the typical small one above the fridge and another full-size standing freezer downstairs. The latter was always packed with bags and bags of *gougères*, small French cheese puffs made of choux pastry.

Keavy's mother, Bridget, always stressed the importance of having these on hand in case a surprise guest showed up at the door. In a pinch, she could pop some *gougères* in the oven and have a fancy-tasting but deceptively simple snack to serve.

At the shop, we use the classic *gougère* recipe, but instead of putting the cheese in the dough, we decided to pipe it in the center with lots of fresh dill and Dijon and serve them warm and gooey with more Cheddar on top.

½ cup (120 ml) whole milk

½ cup (1 stick / 115 g) unsalted butter

½ teaspoon kosher salt

1 cup (125 g) unbleached all-purpose flour

4 large eggs

Cheddar-Dijon or Cheddar–Green Chile Filling (see page 180)

1 pound (455 g) Cheddar cheese, sliced into 2-inch (5-cm) squares, ⅛ inch (3 mm) thick

Preheat the oven to 425°F (220°C).

In a large pot, combine ½ cup (120 ml) water, the milk, butter, and salt over medium heat. Wait until the butter melts, then stir in the flour. Mix with a spatula for 2 to 3 minutes, until the batter dries out a bit. Transfer the mixture to the bowl of a stand mixer fitted with the paddle attachment. Mix it on medium speed for about 2 minutes to cool off the batter, then add the eggs, one at a time, until the mixture comes together. The texture should be pretty wet and sticky.

Using a pastry bag fitted with a ½-inch (12-mm) round tip, or a tablespoon, pipe or spoon the batter onto two parchment-lined baking sheets, about 2 inches (5 cm) apart.

Bake until the puffs are golden brown in the cracks, about 14 minutes, rotating them once halfway through. Let the puffs cool completely on the baking sheets. If you don't plan to use them immediately, store them in an airtight container in the freezer for up to 1 month.

When you're ready to serve them, use a paring knife to make a small hole in the bottom of each one. With a pastry bag fitted with a ½-inch (12-mm) round tip, pipe the filling into the puffs. Pop them into a 350°F (175°C) oven for 5 minutes with a small slice of Cheddar on top of each puff.

Makes about
50
puffs; serves
8 to 12

For service, we pipe this filling into the cheese puffs, but behind the scenes, our staff likes to make cheese sandwiches with it or spread it onto crackers as a snack.

In a food processor, blend the dill, Cheddar, cream cheese, sour cream, mustard, and salt until the mixture is smooth. Store in an airtight container in the refrigerator. Mixture will stay fresh for up to 1 week.

CHEDDAR-DIJON FILLING

Makes about 2¼ cups (220 g)

1 cup (50 g) fresh dill

¾ cup (85 g) shredded Cheddar cheese

¼ cup (60 g) cream cheese

¼ cup (60 ml) sour cream

2 teaspoons Dijon mustard

½ teaspoon kosher salt

This filling was invented for a green chile pop-up dinner we had at the shop featuring Allison and her family from New Mexico. There are not many things that go together better than green chile and cheese, so this combination was a no-brainer.

In a food processor, combine the Cheddar, chile, cream cheese, sour cream, and salt until the mixture is smooth. Store in an airtight container in the refrigerator. Mixture will stay fresh for up to 1 week.

NOTE: If you can't get your hands on the real-deal Hatch green chiles, the canned stuff at the grocery store will suffice. Just be sure to add ½ teaspoon cayenne to the mix to give it that extra kick.

CHEDDAR–GREEN CHILE FILLING

Makes about 1¾ cups (280 g)

¾ cup (85 g) shredded Cheddar cheese

½ cup (75 g) chopped hot New Mexican Hatch green chiles (see Note)

¼ cup (60 g) cream cheese

¼ cup (60 ml) sour cream

½ teaspoon kosher salt

Sticky Toffee Trifle

We strongly believe that most desserts should be drenched in caramel sauce. It can be any kind of caramel—boozy, chocolate, spiced. As long as the dessert is totally soaked in it, we're happy. This is why things like sticky toffee pudding and trifles have always appealed to us. In a moment of sheer genius, we decided to combine the two, creating one of our favorite desserts on our menu.

It may be the most complicated recipe we have in this book, but if you decide to tackle it, the end result is so very rewarding, and big enough to serve a party!

Make the cake: Preheat the oven to 350°F (175°C). Grease a 9 by 13-inch (23 by 33-cm) baking pan with oil.

In a medium saucepan over medium-high heat, bring the dates, butter, and 2 cups (480 ml) water to a boil. Remove the pan from the heat and add the baking soda. Using an immersion blender, puree the mixture until mostly smooth, with just a few small chunks of dates remaining in the pot. Blend in the eggs and vanilla, then gently stir in the flour, baking powder, and salt until just combined.

Pour the batter into the prepared pan; bake for about 30 minutes, rotating halfway through, until the cake is set and crusty on top.

RECIPE CONTINUES

For the cake:

Oil, for the pan

12 ounces (340 g) pitted dates

½ cup (1 stick / 115 g) unsalted butter

2 teaspoons baking soda

4 large eggs

1 teaspoon vanilla extract

4 cups (500 g) unbleached all-purpose flour

2 teaspoons baking powder

1 teaspoon kosher salt

2 cups (480 ml) Caramel Bourbon Sauce (page 41)

For the butterscotch pudding:

5 cups (1.2 L) whole milk

½ cup (65 g) cornstarch

4 large eggs

2 tablespoons vanilla extract

½ cup (1 stick / 115 g) unsalted butter

1¾ cups (385 g) firmly packed dark brown sugar

1½ tablespoons kosher salt

For the assembly:

2 quarts (2 L) Whipped Cream (page 45)

2 cups (240 g) Candied Pecans (page 45)

Allow the cake to sit in the pan until cool enough to touch. If not using immediately, wrap the cake and pan in plastic and keep in the freezer for up to 1 month.

STICKY TOFFEE TRIFLE CONTINUED

With clean hands or forks, shred up the cake into chunks, then put it in a large bowl and douse it with the caramel sauce until fully coated.

Make the pudding: In a medium bowl, whisk together the milk and cornstarch and set aside. In a small bowl, whisk together the eggs and vanilla and set aside.

In a medium saucepan, melt the butter over medium heat. Add the brown sugar and stir until the sugar is totally coated with butter, then add the salt. When the sugar starts to boil, add the milk and cornstarch mixture. Stir well with a whisk, then add the egg mixture in a thin stream, whisking constantly while pouring it. Continue stirring with a whisk until the mixture has thickened; you should see whisk marks as you stir, and it should coat the back of a spoon. Remove the pudding from the heat, pour it through a sieve into a bowl or onto a baking sheet, wrap it in plastic (press the plastic against the surface of the pudding), and place it in the refrigerator to cool.

Assemble the trifle: In a large punch bowl, scatter half of the chunks of the date cake (you can just grab them with your hands or scoop with a spoon), then top with half of the butterscotch pudding, then 1 quart (960 ml) of the whipped cream, and half of the pecans. Repeat the process a second time. To serve, scoop the trifle into bowls. This should be eaten immediately, as it doesn't store well once assembled.

Serves 30 to 40

Makes
2
cakes; serves
8 to 12

Tequila King Cake

When you run a bakery that also happens to be a bar, a lot of people reach out to you for boozy versions of classic desserts. Espolón Tequila did just that for the launch of their añejo tequila, asking us to come up with a booze-infused version of the king cake. It's a classic treat usually served at Mardi Gras in New Orleans, and for Epiphany—or Three Kings' Day—every January. (Legend says if you find the baby hidden in your slice, you'll have good luck all year!) They also asked us to pair it with a cocktail, and we came up with the aptly named La Epifanía (page 198). Try them together; it's sure to be a revelation!

Make the dough: In a saucepan over medium heat, heat the milk until scalded, then remove it from the heat and stir in the butter. Allow the mixture to cool to room temperature.

In the bowl of a stand mixer fitted with the dough hook attachment, stir together the yeast, warm water, and 1 teaspoon of the sugar. Let the mixture stand for about 10 minutes.

When the yeast mixture is spongy, stir in the cooled milk mixture. Whisk in the eggs, then stir in the remaining ½ cup (100 g) of the sugar, the salt, and nutmeg. Beat the flour into the mixture on low speed, 1 cup (125 g) at a time, then beat on medium until the dough pulls together and away from the sides of the bowl.

Turn the dough out onto a lightly floured surface and knead it for about 10 minutes, until it is smooth and elastic. Lightly oil a large bowl, place the dough in the bowl, and turn to coat it with oil. Cover the bowl with a damp cloth or plastic wrap and let the dough rise in a warm place until doubled in volume, about 2 hours.

For the dough:

1 cup (240 ml) whole milk

½ cup (1 stick / 115 g) unsalted butter

2 packets (4½ teaspoons) active dry yeast

⅔ cup (160 ml) warm water

½ cup (100 g) plus 1 teaspoon sugar

2 large eggs

½ teaspoon kosher salt

¼ teaspoon freshly grated nutmeg

5½ cups (690 g) unbleached all-purpose flour, plus more for dusting

Vegetable oil, for the bowl

RECIPE CONTINUES

When the dough has risen, punch it down and divide it in half.

Line two rimmed half baking sheets (13 by 18 inches / 33 by 46 cm) with parchment paper.

Make the filling: In a small bowl, combine the brown sugar, lime zest, and orange zest. Set aside.

On a floured surface, roll each dough half out into a large rectangle (approximately 10 by 16 inches / 25 by 40.5 cm). Brush each rectangle with half of the melted butter and sprinkle the brown sugar mixture evenly over both. Carefully roll up each rectangle from a long edge to create two long tubes. Seal the seams.

Bring the ends of each roll together to form two oval rings and pinch the ends to seal them together. Place each ring on a prepared baking sheet. With a knife, make cuts one-third of the way through the rings at 1-inch (2.5-cm) intervals. Let the cakes rise, lightly covered, in a warm spot until doubled in size, about 45 minutes.

Preheat the oven to 350°F (175°C).

Bake the cakes for 30 minutes, until dark golden brown on top. While the cakes are still warm but no longer hot, push one baby (if using) up through the bottom of each cake. Put on wire racks to cool.

Make the glaze: In a medium bowl, mix together the confectioners' sugar, tequila, ½ cup (120 ml) water, and the lime and orange zests. Once the cakes are cool, spoon the glaze evenly over the top of each cake. While the icing is still wet, sprinkle sanding sugar over the top. Store in an airtight container at room temperature for up to 2 days.

TEQUILA KING
CAKE CONTINUED

For the filling:

2 cups (440 g) firmly packed dark brown sugar

Zest of 1 lime

Zest of ½ orange

1 cup (2 sticks / 225 g) unsalted butter, melted

2 small food-safe plastic babies (optional; these can be purchased online and at bakery supply stores)

For the glaze and topping:

1 pound (455 g) confectioners' sugar

¼ cup (60 ml) añejo tequila

Zest of ½ lime

Zest of ½ orange

White sanding sugar, for garnish (or the colors of your choice)

Brownie Sundae

Like all good sundaes, this is a big old mess: It's a warm gooey brownie on the bottom soaking in loads of hot fudge and caramel sauce, topped with three large scoops of ice cream, mountains of whipped cream, and, of course, three cherries. It should be served with extra napkins and a few spoons.

Preheat the oven to 350°F (175°C).

Heat the brownie on a small baking sheet until warmed through, about 5 minutes. Lay the brownie on the bottom of a sundae boat or bowl. Pour half of each of the hot fudge and caramel sauce over the brownie, then top with the ice cream. Top the ice cream with the rest of the hot fudge and caramel sauce, the whipped cream, toffee bits, and cherries.

Serves 1 to 2, depending on your appetite!

1 Brownie (page 189)

½ cup (120 ml) Hot Fudge (page 39)

½ cup (120 ml) Classic Caramel Sauce (page 40)

3 scoops vanilla ice cream

¼ cup (25 g) Crushed Toffee bits (page 44)

½ cup (120 ml) Whipped Cream (page 45)

3 maraschino cherries (we use Fabbri)

We use these brownies for our Brownie Sundae (page 181), but they are no slouch on their own. They are a dense, rich, and gooey style of brownie as opposed to cakey. We use three different types of chocolate: cocoa powder, melted bittersweet, and bittersweet chocolate chips, as well as instant espresso and brown sugar to create a rich chocolate flavor without making it too sweet. As with the Chocolate Cupcakes (page 22), these brownies are best when they are slightly underbaked.

Preheat the oven to 350°F (175°C). Grease a 9 by 13-inch (23 by 33-inch) baking pan.

In a medium bowl, combine the flour, cocoa powder, espresso powder, and salt and set aside.

In the bowl of a stand mixer fitted with the whisk attachment, cream together both sugars and the melted butter until fluffy, about 1 minute. With the mixer on medium speed, slowly add the eggs and vanilla. Turn the mixer down to the lowest speed and slowly add the flour mixture. Add the melted chocolate and chocolate chips and mix on low speed until just combined. Scrape the batter into the prepared pan and smooth the top.

Bake for 15 to 20 minutes, rotating once halfway through, until the brownies are set and crackly on top. Allow them to cool completely before cutting. Cut into six equal rectangles, then store in an airtight container at room temperature. If not eaten within a few days, the brownies will keep in the freezer for up to a month.

BROWNIES

Makes 6 brownies; enough for 6 Brownie Sundaes (page 187)

1 cup (125 g) unbleached all-purpose flour

½ cup (50 g) unsweetened cocoa powder

1 teaspoon instant espresso powder

1 teaspoon kosher salt

1 cup (200 g) granulated sugar

½ cup (110 g) firmly packed dark brown sugar

1 cup (2 sticks / 225 g) unsalted butter, melted

4 large eggs

1 teaspoon vanilla extract

4 ounces (115 g) chopped bittersweet chocolate, melted

¾ cup (130 g) bittersweet chocolate chips

The Rockford Peaches

This drink gets its name from one of our favorite movies ever—*A League of Their Own*. It's an incredibly easy drink to make and is a very summery riff on a whiskey sour. It would be super delicious paired with something spicy like our Dark & Stormy Caramel Corn or Green Chile Margarita Caramel Corn (pages 207 and 209).

Fill a cocktail shaker with ice. Measure the rye, peach liqueur, lemon juice, and bitters into it. Shake well and strain the drink into a glass over fresh ice. Garnish with the lemon wheel.

Ice cubes

2 ounces (60 ml) rye whiskey (we use Old Overholt)

1 ounce peach liqueur (we use Giffard Crème de Pêche de Vigne)

½ ounce fresh lemon juice

2 dashes Fee's Aromatic Bitters

Thinly sliced lemon wheel, for garnish

Serves 1

F*ck the Pain Away

For one of our monthly pop-up dinners, our friends Lauren and Flannery of bigLITTLE Get Together did an all-peach menu, and we were tasked with coming up with complementary desserts and cocktails. This riff on the classic painkiller cocktail takes its name from one of our favorite songs ever, by the brilliant musician and performance artist Peaches. It's powerful and complex, just like her!

Fill a cocktail shaker with ice. Measure the white rum, peach liqueur, peach puree, orange juice, overproof rum, coconut cream, and lime juice into it. Shake and strain the liquid into a collins glass. Fill it with ice and garnish with the peach wedge, lime wheel, umbrella, and a straw.

NOTE: You can find peach puree in the freezer section of some gourmet grocery stores, but to make your own, just puree the flesh of a whole peach with 1 tablespoon water.

To make the coconut cream, combine equal parts Coco Lopez and coconut milk in a blender and puree until smooth.

Serves 1

Ice cubes

1 ounce white rum (we use Plantation 3 Star)

1 ounce peach liqueur (we use Giffard Crème de Pêche de Vigne)

1 ounce peach puree (see Note)

1 ounce fresh orange juice

½ ounce dark overproof rum (above 125 proof; we use Plantation)

½ ounce coconut cream (see Note)

¼ ounce fresh lime juice

Peach wedge, lime wheel, and cocktail umbrella, for garnish

Honeychile Rider

Before we even opened our doors, we were invited to participate in the Queen Bee Cocktail Classic as part of NYC Honey Week, an annual event celebrating the honeybee. We were challenged to create a cocktail incorporating local honey, and we immediately reached out to our friend Mike of Mike's Hot Honey. If you've never tried his ingenious creation, it's local honey infused with a wickedly delicious blend of chiles, and it's good on *everything*, from pizza to ice cream. It's especially great in this cocktail, and a big part of the reason that we won the Queen Bee Cocktail Classic!

Fill a cocktail shaker with ice. Measure the gin, passion fruit puree, honey simple syrup, lemon juice, and simple syrup into it. Shake well, then strain the liquid over fresh ice in a rocks glass. Top with the bitters.

Serves 1

Ice cubes

1½ ounces gin (we like Dorothy Parker from New York Distilling Company for this)

½ ounce passion fruit puree (see Note, page 92)

½ ounce Hot Honey Simple Syrup (page 48)

½ ounce fresh lemon juice, strained

¼ ounce Simplest Simple Syrup (page 47)

5 drops Bittermens 'Elemakule Tiki Bitters

Japanese Scot

When we started making orgeat (almond syrup) in-house, we looked for as many drinks as we could to put it in; it's so delicious! Scotch is right there in our name, so people often look to us for a good selection of Scotch whiskies and Scotch-based cocktails. We decided to try a riff on the classic Japanese Cocktail, made with Scotch instead of cognac. It's a little smoky, a little nutty, and a lot smooth—it's a winner!

In a mixing glass filled with ice, stir together the Scotch, orgeat, and bitters. Strain them into a chilled cordial glass and garnish with the lemon peel.

Serves 1

Ice cubes

2 ounces (60 ml) blended Scotch

½ ounce Orgeat (page 53)

2 dashes Fee's Aromatic Bitters

Lemon peel, for garnish

Rita & Bernie

This cocktail is named for Allison's favorite great-aunt and great-uncle, two of her favorite people in the world. They credit their longevity (Bernie is over one hundred years old, and Rita is catching up) to their lust for life, love of travel, and daily tipple of Scotch whisky. We already created a hot version of a cocktail incorporating both butter and scotch (the Hot Buttered Scotch, page 146), but we also wanted to do a cold version for the warmer months. By fat-washing the Scotch (you can read more about the technique on page 55), we get all of the nutty, creamy flavor of brown butter without any greasiness. This is a riff on a classic Rob Roy cocktail, which was en vogue back in the day when Rita and Bernie were first courting! Be sure to use a good single malt for this, so the richness of the brown butter doesn't overpower the flavor of the Scotch.

Ice cubes

2 ounces (60 ml) Brown Butter Scotch (page 55)

1 ounce Cardamaro (see Note)

3 dashes Angostura bitters

Maraschino cherry (we use Fabbri), for garnish

In an ice-filled mixing glass, stir the Scotch, Cardamaro, and bitters until well chilled, about 20 seconds. Strain them into a chilled cocktail glass and garnish with the cherry.

NOTE: Cardamaro is a wine-based amaro, sort of a cross between an amaro and a vermouth, and it gives the perfect dry/bitter balance to this cocktail. Store it in the refrigerator once it's opened to keep it fresh!

Serves 1

Ariel's Song

To say we were excited to add a frozen drink to our menu is an understatement. If we could have all our drinks served to us frozen in a tiki glass with an umbrella and a twisty straw, we would. With three ounces of booze, this drink is no slouch, and just like the Disney character of the same name, you might lose your voice after drinking one (or three!) of these in a night.

In a blender, combine the orange juice, orgeat, lime juice, all three rums, Frangelico, and triple sec with approximately 12 ice cubes (fill to the three-quarter mark on the blender). Blend until totally smooth and serve in your favorite tiki mug. Garnish with a skewer loaded with an orange wedge, lime wheel, and cherry, then add a cocktail umbrella and a straw.

Serves 1

2 ounces (60 ml) fresh orange juice

1 ounce Orgeat (page 53)

¾ ounce fresh lime juice

1 ounce white rum

½ ounce spiced rum (we use Old New Orleans Cajun Spiced Rum)

½ ounce Gosling's Black Seal Rum

½ ounce Frangelico liqueur

½ ounce triple sec

Ice cubes

Orange wedge, lime wheel, and maraschino cherry, for garnish

La Epifanía

This was the first drink we ever sold at Butter & Scotch, as a part of a sneak-peek promotion we did before we opened. Even though it never made it onto the opening menu, we still have regulars coming back to order it to this day. As with any recipe with so few ingredients, quality is important, so get your hands on some really good tequila—we love Espolón's añejo for this cocktail.

In a mixing glass filled with ice, stir together the tequila, ginger-lime syrup, and bitters until chilled. Strain the mixture into a chilled rocks glass and garnish with a skewer of candied ginger.

Serves 1

Ice cubes

2 ounces (60 ml) añejo tequila (we use Espolón)

½ ounce Ginger-Lime Simple Syrup (recipe follows)

6 drops Bittermens 'Elemakule Tiki Bitters

Candied ginger, for garnish

In a small saucepan, heat the sugar, ginger, and lime zest with ¼ cup (60 ml) water over medium heat until the sugar has dissolved. Allow the zest to steep for 30 minutes, then strain and discard the solids. The syrup keeps for up to 1 month in the fridge.

GINGER-LIME SIMPLE SYRUP

Makes ½ cup (120 ml)

¼ cup (50 g) sugar
½ teaspoon ground ginger
Zest of ½ lime

Late Night

Late night at Butter & Scotch may be our **favorite** time
at the shop: Patrons amped up on sugar begin belting
out the words to our bar manager Haley's infamous nineties mix;
bakers emerge from the kitchen to do Disco Nap **shots** with the
bartenders; and regulars begin reaching behind the bar for the
secret stash of cigarettes kept in the "Bar Tools" cabinet.
Orders for Pimento Cheese and Triscuits and Sesame-Chile Popcorn fly
out the window, giving **inebriated** patrons much-needed
salty snacks to soak up the booze. And our "artisanal"
Jell-Ohh Shots help birthday parties relive their college days
without feeling too shameful. It's the perfect blend of
childlike excitement and anarchy, and it's what makes
being in the shop such an **electric** experience.

Pimento Cheese

It's hard to find a cheese spread that we don't like, but this tops them all. It's creamy from the mayo, spicy from the Tabasco, and tangy with a touch of sweetness from the peppers. It's got everything that a good cheese dip needs. At the shop, we serve it in a little cup with a pile of Triscuits. This combination has served as our dinner more times than we care to admit.

In a food processor, blend the cheese, mayonnaise, half of the pimentos, the Tabasco, cayenne, salt, and paprika. Once the mixture comes together and has a slightly lumpy, but mostly smooth texture, fold in the remaining half of the pimentos. Taste to check the spice level, and if you like more heat, add more Tabasco to taste. Store in an airtight container in the fridge for up to 1 week.

Serve the spread with crackers.

Makes 4 cups (960 ml)

½ pound (225 g) sharp Cheddar cheese, cubed

½ cup (120 ml) mayonnaise

1 cup (140 g) diced pimento peppers, drained

About 1 tablespoon Tabasco sauce

¾ teaspoon cayenne

½ teaspoon kosher salt

¼ teaspoon paprika

Triscuits or Ritz crackers, for serving

Sesame-Chile Popcorn

For one of our savory snacks at Butter & Scotch, we wanted to offer an option that would appeal to everyone, including those avoiding dairy and gluten. This is a delicious, spicy, endlessly snackable popcorn (and we serve *big* bowls of it) that's sure to please a crowd and keep you drinking!

2 tablespoons canola oil

¼ cup (50 g) popcorn kernels

2 tablespoons Sesame-Chile Oil (page 204)

½ teaspoon red pepper flakes

¾ teaspoon kosher salt

In a large pot, heat the canola oil over medium-high heat until it shimmers and coats the bottom of the pot. Add the popcorn kernels and cover, shaking the pot frequently. The popcorn will start to pop. When you hear it slow down, turn off the heat and keep shaking the pot until you only hear the occasional pop.

Pour the popcorn into a large bowl, drizzle with the sesame-chile oil, sprinkle over the red pepper flakes and salt, and toss well to coat. Serve hot!

Serves 1 to 2

SESAME-CHILE OIL

Makes 1 cup (240 ml)

1 cup (240 ml) sesame oil
1 ancho chile, roughly chopped

In a small pot, heat the oil over low heat until just hot.
Remove it from the heat, add the chile, and pour the mixture into
a heatproof airtight container. Allow the oil to infuse for
at least 2 hours. It can infuse for up to 1 week for added
intensity and heat. Strain out the chile and store at room
temperature for up to 1 month.

COCKTAIL CARAMEL CORNS

If there is one product that truly embodies our name and brand, this is it: snacky, salty, sweet caramel corn designed to taste like different cocktails. These are all so addictive that we're not allowed to bring them home anymore. And don't ask us which one's our favorite, because we will go around in circles trying to decide.

Dark & Stormy Caramel Corn

This is a flavor joyride: The lime zest hits you right away, while the ginger comes on strong at the end. It's really important to use fresh ginger when making this caramel corn; the flavor is so much brighter and gives the corn a little kick. We also use Gosling's Black Seal Rum, which is the trademark rum of all Dark & Stormy cocktails, and gives it that creamy vanilla note that perfectly complements the other bold flavors happening here.

Preheat the oven to 325°F (165°C). Grease two rimmed metal baking sheets and set aside.

In a large heavy-bottomed pot, heat the sugar, butter, and corn syrup over medium-high, stirring until they are well incorporated. Cook the mixture until you smell the caramelized sugar and see it turn a light amber/beige color. Remove the pot from the heat and whisk in the baking soda. Then whisk in the rum, ginger, salt, and lime zest (be careful; the caramel will release a lot of steam, so guard your hands). When all the ingredients are incorporated, fold in the popcorn using a heatproof spatula or wooden spoon. Keep folding, pulling caramel up from the bottom and over the popcorn, until it is well coated.

Spread the popcorn out on the baking sheets and bake for 20 minutes, pulling it out every 5 minutes to fold and toss to better coat the popcorn with caramel. Remove the popcorn from the oven to cool completely (this takes about 20 minutes), then serve or seal in airtight bags.

The caramel corn will last for up to 5 weeks when kept in an airtight bag away from humidity.

1 cup (200 g) sugar

½ cup (1 stick / 115 g) unsalted butter

¼ cup (60 ml) light corn syrup (see Note, page 39)

¼ teaspoon baking soda

3 tablespoons Gosling's Black Seal Rum

1 tablespoon grated peeled fresh ginger

2 teaspoons kosher salt

Zest of 1 lime

14 cups (90 g) popped popcorn (from about ½ cup / 100 g kernels)

**Makes approximately
14 cups (210 g)**

Hot Toddy Caramel Corn

Toddies may be cold-weather drinks, but this caramel corn is great to snack on all year-round. Our favorite part about this is the contrast of the dark bourbon, honey, and cinnamon flavors with the bright flavor of lemon zest.

Preheat the oven to 325° F (165°C). Grease two rimmed metal baking sheets and set aside.

In a large heavy-bottomed pot, heat the sugar, butter, and honey over medium-high, stirring until they are well incorporated. Cook the mixture until you smell the caramelized sugar and see it turn a light amber/beige color. Remove the pot from the heat and whisk in the baking soda. Then whisk in the bourbon, salt, lemon zest, and cinnamon (be careful, the caramel will release a lot of steam, so guard your hands). When all the ingredients are incorporated, fold in the popcorn using a heatproof spatula or wooden spoon. Keep folding, pulling caramel up from the bottom and over the popcorn, until it is well coated.

Spread the popcorn out on the baking sheets and bake for 20 minutes, pulling it out every 5 minutes to fold and toss to better coat the popcorn with caramel. Remove from the oven and let cool completely (this takes about 20 minutes), then serve or seal in airtight bags.

The caramel corn will last for up to 5 weeks when kept in an airtight bag away from humidity.

Makes approximately 14 cups (210 g)

1 cup (200 g) sugar

½ cup (1 stick / 115 g) unsalted butter

¼ cup (60 ml) clover honey

¼ teaspoon baking soda

3 tablespoons bourbon

2 teaspoons kosher salt

Zest of 1 lemon

1½ teaspoons ground cinnamon

14 cups (90 g) popped popcorn (from about ½ cup / 100 g of kernels)

Green Chile Margarita Caramel Corn

We care so deeply about real Hatch peppers that we've turned our New Mexican friends into green-chile mules. Every time someone goes home to visit, they know the drill: Buy at least ten pounds of frozen chiles for Keavy and Allison!

If you can't find the real stuff, though, you can buy the roasted green chiles found in cans at your local supermarket. Just make sure to double the amount of cayenne.

Preheat the oven to 325° F (165°C). Grease two rimmed metal baking sheets and set aside.

In a large heavy-bottomed pot, heat the sugar, butter, and corn syrup over medium-high, stirring until they are well incorporated. Cook the mixture until you smell the caramelized sugar and see it turn a light amber/beige color. Remove the pot from the heat and whisk in the baking soda. Then whisk in the tequila, chile, salt, cayenne, and lime zest (be careful; the caramel will release a lot of steam, so guard your hands). When all the ingredients are incorporated, fold in the popcorn using a heatproof spatula or wooden spoon. Keep folding, pulling caramel up from the bottom and over the popcorn, until it is well coated.

Spread the popcorn out on the baking sheets and bake for 20 minutes, pulling it out every 5 minutes to fold and toss to better coat the popcorn with caramel. Remove the popcorn from the oven to cool completely (this takes about 20 minutes), then serve or seal in airtight bags.

The caramel corn will last for up to 5 weeks when kept in an airtight bag away from humidity.

1 cup (200 g) sugar

½ cup (1 stick / 115 g) unsalted butter

¼ cup (60 ml) light corn syrup (see Note, page 39)

¼ teaspoon baking soda

3 tablespoons silver tequila

2 tablespoons chopped green chile

2 teaspoons kosher salt

1 teaspoon cayenne

Zest of 1 lime

14 cups (90 g) popped popcorn (from about ½ cup / 100 g kernels)

Makes approximately 14 cups (210 g)

BOOZY SHAKES

There's not a whole lot you can do to improve on a milkshake—it's one of the most perfect desserts around. But we think that adding booze to it might just make it even better. At Butter & Scotch, you can add a shot of any booze to any shake, but we've also created some special shakes that are a bit more complex, drawing from classic (and not-so-classic) cocktails. Blend one up and we think you'll believe the hype.

The Nameshake

We wanted to create a shake inspired by our name, and came up with this sweet and smoky concoction—it's definitely one of our favorites!

In a blender, blend the ice cream, Scotch, and caramel sauce together until smooth. Pour the shake into a parfait or pint glass and garnish with whipped cream, a drizzle of caramel, and a spoonful of crushed toffee. Serve with a straw.

4 scoops vanilla ice cream

2 ounces (60 ml) blended Scotch whisky (we use Monkey Shoulder)

2 tablespoons Classic Caramel Sauce (page 40), plus more for garnish

Whipped Cream (page 45), for garnish

Crushed Toffee bits (page 44), for garnish

Serves 1

El Duderino

"Let me explain something to you. I am not Mr. Lebowski.
You're Mr. Lebowski. I'm the Dude. So that's what you call me. You know,
that or, uh, His Dudeness, or uh, Duder, or El Duderino if you're
not into the whole brevity thing."

—THE DUDE, FROM *THE BIG LEBOWSKI*

Yeah, we love *The Big Lebowski*. And we love milkshakes. And we love White Russians (page 168). So this is a White Russian milkshake named for our favorite Dude.

In a blender, blend the ice cream, vodka, and Kahlúa together until smooth. Pour the shake into a parfait or pint glass and garnish with whipped cream and chocolate-covered espresso beans, if using. Serve with a straw.

Serves 1

4 scoops coffee ice cream

2 ounces (60 ml) vodka (we use Reyka)

1 ounce Kahlúa liqueur

Whipped Cream (page 45), for garnish

Chocolate-covered espresso beans, for garnish (optional)

Rock & Rye

There's a fantastic distillery here in Brooklyn called New York Distilling Company. It's owned by Allen Katz, respected barman and creator of delicious small-batch spirits. We use his Dorothy Parker gin in our Honeychile Rider cocktail (page 192) and his Rock & Rye is amazing in this shake and on its own (it's basically an old fashioned cocktail in a bottle). Made by infusing young rye whiskey with rock candy, sour cherries, orange peel, and cinnamon, it's complex, smooth, and bright.

4 scoops coffee ice cream

2 ounces (60 ml) Mister Katz's Rock & Rye

1 ounce sour cherry puree (see Sources, page 230)

Whipped Cream (page 45), for garnish

Maraschino cherry (we use Fabbri), for garnish

In a blender, blend the ice cream, Rock & Rye, and sour cherry puree until smooth. Pour the shake into a parfait or pint glass and garnish with whipped cream and a cherry. Serve with a straw.

Serves 1

If You Like Piña Coladas

Please don't hate us for getting that song stuck in your head! Just make one of these and succumb to the smooth sounds of Jimmy Buffet. At Butter & Scotch, we make this with a crazy-delicious dairy-free (!) coconut ice cream from our friends at Blue Marble Organic Ice Cream, so it's totally vegan (but you wouldn't know it!).

In a blender, blend the ice cream, rum, and pineapple chunks until smooth. Pour the shake into a parfait or pint glass and garnish with a bamboo skewer of pineapple and a cherry, and maybe an umbrella for kicks—make it tiki!

4 scoops coconut ice cream

2 ounces (60 ml) white rum

¼ cup (40 g) canned pineapple chunks, drained

Fresh pineapple wedge and spears, for garnish

Maraschino cherry (we use Fabbri), for garnish

Serves 1

Dewhopper

The grasshopper is one of those classic cocktails that's almost a dessert already. We decided to officially bring it over into the sweets realm and add some Irish whiskey for an extra kick! It's chocolatey-minty goodness, and deceptively potent.

In a blender, blend the ice cream, whiskey, crème de menthe, and crème de cacao until smooth. Pour the shake into a parfait or pint glass and garnish with whipped cream and dark chocolate shavings. Serve with a straw.

Serves 1

4 scoops vanilla ice cream

1 ounce Irish whiskey (we use Tullamore D.E.W.)

½ ounce green crème de menthe

½ ounce clear crème de cacao

Whipped Cream (page 45), for garnish

Dark chocolate shavings, for garnish

Ramos
Gin Fizz

The Ramos gin fizz has always been a favorite of mine, so when it occurred to me to incorporate it into our ice cream cocktail selections, I couldn't wait. As you can imagine, I had such fun during the R&D phase of this cocktail. After many iterations, we settled on this recipe. I'm especially happy with the texture and extra orange punch provided by the marmalade, while still keeping it traditional with the orange flower water. It's such a delicious variation on this classic. —Jen Marshall, Opening Beverage Director & All-Around Rad Chick

4 scoops vanilla ice cream

1½ ounces dry gin (we use Bulldog, but any good dry gin will do)

½ ounce fresh lime juice

½ ounce orange flower water

1 tablespoon orange marmalade

Whipped Cream (page 45), for garnish

Orange zest, for garnish (optional)

In a blender, blend the ice cream, gin, lime juice, orange flower water, and marmalade until smooth. Pour the shake into a parfait or pint glass and garnish with whipped cream and orange zest, if using. Serve with a straw.

Serves 1

Disco Nap

We work late nights and long hours, and sometimes we need a little fuel to keep our energy up. That's where the Disco Nap comes in. We take some good tequila (the only booze known to act as a stimulant, rather than a depressant), infuse it with strong coffee, and then mix it with a little amaro to smooth it out. We serve it up in our favorite little cowboy boot shot glasses and keep the party going!

Stir the coffee into the tequila. Store it overnight at room temperature in an airtight container. Strain the liquid through a strainer lined with a coffee filter. Combine it with the amaro and refrigerate until ready to serve, or up to 1 month. Pour doses into your favorite shot glasses at your next party. Cheers!

Makes about 1½ cups (360 ml); serves 8

1 ounce (30 g) coarsely ground dark-roast coffee beans

8 ounces (240 ml) Altos Reposado Tequila

4 ounces (120 ml) Montenegro amaro

JELL-OHH SHOTS

Typically served in plastic cups at frat parties, Jell-O shots get a bad rap. But we *love* Jell-O shots, and when made right, they can be incredibly fun and tasty.

In the following pages are some tried-and-true recipes that we love, but when it comes to Jell-Ohh Shots, the world is your oyster! Follow the process and ratios (1½ teaspoons unflavored powdered gelatin to 1 cup / 240 ml liquid) and you can easily create your own cocktail-inspired Jell-Ohh Shot.

Blood & Sand

This is Keavy's personal favorite and has been around for the longest. If you can't find blood oranges, fear not, these are just as delicious with regular juicing oranges.

Slice each blood orange in half and juice it. Set the juice aside. (You'll need ¼ cup / 60 ml juice. Drink any extra you might get!). Carefully scoop out and discard the pith and remaining flesh from the juiced orange halves.

Pour the orange juice into a saucepan and sprinkle the gelatin over the top. Allow it to bloom for at least 1 minute. Heat it gently over low heat until the gelatin dissolves, then remove it from the heat and stir in the vermouth, cherry Heering, Scotch, and 2 tablespoons water.

Pour the mixture into the prepared orange halves (keep them level and fill them as much as possible) and refrigerate until set, about 30 minutes.

Slice the shots in half to make wedges. Eat them right out of the orange rinds!

4 large blood oranges

1½ teaspoons unflavored powdered gelatin

2 ounces (60 ml) sweet vermouth

2 ounces (60 ml) Cherry Heering liqueur

2 ounces (60 ml) blended Scotch whiskey (we use Monkey Shoulder)

Teaches of Peaches

We created these for the second annual Queen Bee Cocktail Classic, and as we did the year before, we took home the Fan Favorite award for these sweet, spicy, fruity gems. Typically, we serve our Jell-Ohh Shots in citrus rinds, but these are served in the actual peach, meaning you can eat the whole thing!

Pour the rum, peach puree, peach liqueur, orange juice, coconut cream, lime juice, simple syrup, and 1 ounce water into a saucepan. Sprinkle over the gelatin and allow it to bloom for at least 1 minute. Heat the mixture gently over low heat until the gelatin just dissolves, then remove it from the heat.

Pour the mixture into the peach halves (keep them level and fill them as much as possible) and refrigerate until set, at least 30 minutes.

Slice the peach halves in half to make wedges, and serve.

NOTE: To prep the peach halves, use a melon baller to carefully scoop out the flesh. Save the flesh for compote, jam, or peach puree (see Note, page 191).

3 ounces (90 ml) Owney's Rum

2 ounces (60 ml) peach puree (see note, page 191)

2 ounces (60 ml) peach liqueur (we use Giffard Crème de Pêche de Vigne)

2 ounces (60 ml) fresh orange juice

1 ounce coconut cream (see Note, page 191)

1 ounce fresh lime juice

1 ounce Hot Honey Simple Syrup (page 48)

2 teaspoons gelatin

4 peaches, halved and pitted, with most of the flesh scooped out (see Note)

Makes

16

shots

Rum Punch

Whenever a customer orders this shot at the bar, we can't help but say it right back to them: "Rrrrrum punch," rolling our r's and with a British accent just like Mary Poppins. Maybe it's the nostalgia that makes this so popular, or maybe it's just because it's freakin' delicious. It's hard to taste the booze in this one, so be careful!

Pour the pineapple juice, 1 ounce of the orange juice (you can drink the rest), and the lime juice into a saucepan and sprinkle the gelatin over the top. Allow it to bloom for at least 1 minute. Heat it gently over low heat until the gelatin dissolves, then remove it from the heat and stir in the rum, triple sec, and 1 ounce water.

Pour the mixture into the prepared orange halves (keep them level and fill them as much as possible) and refrigerate until set, about 30 minutes.

Slice the shots in half to make wedges. Eat them right out of the orange rinds!

2 ounces (60 ml) pineapple juice

4 oranges, halved and juiced, with the juice reserved and pulp and flesh scooped out

½ ounce fresh lime juice

1½ teaspoons unflavored powdered gelatin

3 ounces (90 ml) El Dorado white rum

1 ounce triple sec

Makes 16 shots

Eff You, V-Day

We created these for our shop's first Valentine's Day. When customers came in, they had the choice of an adorable mini-cupcake with frosting shaped like a pretty pink rose, or a face-cringing bitter Jell-Ohh Shot that was dyed jet-black. Each item represented how one of us felt about Valentine's Day: Allison repping the mini-cupcake and Keavy repping the Jell-Ohh Shot.

2 grapefruits

¾ ounce Simplest Simple Syrup (page 47)

1 teaspoon unflavored powdered gelatin

1½ ounces Reyka vodka

¼ ounce Fernet Branca

Slice each grapefruit in half and juice it. Set 2 tablespoons of the juice aside (you can drink the rest). Carefully scoop out and discard the pith and remaining flesh from the juiced grapefruit halves.

Pour the 2 tablespoons of grapefruit juice and the simple syrup into a saucepan and sprinkle the gelatin over the top. Allow it to bloom for at least 1 minute. Heat it gently over low heat until the gelatin dissolves, then remove it from the heat and stir in the vodka and Fernet.

Pour the liquid into the prepared grapefruit halves (keep them level and fill them as much as possible) and refrigerate until set, at least 30 minutes.

Slice the shots in half, then in half again, to make 4 wedges per grapefruit half. Eat them right out of the rinds!

Makes 16 shots

Aviation

A well-made Aviation is one of Allison's favorite cocktails, so it was a no-brainer when adding it as a Jell-Ohh Shot to our menu. We put just a touch of purple dye into the mix, which creates a beautiful lavender hue that complements the bright-yellow lemon rind perfectly.

Slice each lemon in half and juice it. Set 2 ounces (60 ml) fresh lemon juice aside (you can use the rest for something else). Carefully scoop out and discard the pith and remaining flesh from the juiced lemon halves.

Pour the lemon juice and simple syrup into a saucepan and sprinkle the gelatin over the top. Allow it to bloom for at least 1 minute. Heat it gently over low heat until the gelatin dissolves, then remove it from the heat and stir in the gin, maraschino liqueur, crème de violette, and 1½ ounces water. Stir in the dye, if using.

Pour the liquid into the prepared lemon halves (keep them level and fill them as much as possible) and refrigerate until set, at least 30 minutes.

Slice the shots in half to make wedges. Eat them right out of the rinds!

Makes 16 shots

4 lemons

¼ ounce Simplest Simple Syrup (page 47)

1½ teaspoons unflavored powdered gelatin

4½ ounces (135 ml) dry gin (we use Bulldog)

1½ ounces Luxardo Maraschino Liqueur

½ ounce Crème de Violette

1 drop purple food dye (optional)

Sazerac

This New-Orleans-classic-turned-Jell-Ohh-Shot is not for the faint of heart, as it is all booze. Since there is no glass for these, in lieu of the traditional absinthe "rinse," we add the tiniest bit straight to the mixture, giving it a wonderful fennel-y aftertaste.

Slice each lemon in half and juice it (you can use the juice for something else). Carefully scoop out and discard the pith and remaining flesh from the juiced lemon halves.

In a saucepan, combine the simple syrup and 1½ ounces water and sprinkle the gelatin over the top. Allow it to bloom for at least 1 minute. Heat it gently over low heat until the gelatin dissolves, then remove it from the heat and stir in the whiskey, absinthe, and bitters.

Pour the liquid into the prepared lemon halves (keep them level and fill them as much as possible), and refrigerate until set, about 30 minutes.

Slice the shots in half to make wedges. Eat them right out of the rinds!

4 lemons

¾ ounce Simplest Simple Syrup (page 47)

1½ teaspoons unflavored powdered gelatin

6 ounces (180 ml) rye whiskey

¼ ounce absinthe

6 dashes Peychaud's bitters

4 dashes Angostura bitters

Makes 16 shots

TECHNIQUES

Canning

Here are some basic guidelines to use if you're planning to preserve jams, jellies, or marmalades. It's a great way to stretch the best of each season's harvest so you can enjoy them year-round! A big hat-tip to our friend Camilla Wynne of Preservation Society, whose book has been a great resource for all things canning and preserving.

- Use thick-walled glass jars made for canning, with new snap lids.
- Wash your jars, lids, and bands in hot, soapy water or the dishwasher.
- Submerge the jars in a large pot of simmering water, with a metal rack or dish towel at the bottom, and keep them there until it's time to fill them with preserves. Use this same pot for canning.
- When your preserves are ready, carefully remove the hot jars from the water and drain them well (there are special canning tongs that are great for this). Fill the jars, leaving about ½ inch (12 mm) headspace at the top. Remove any air bubbles by stirring the contents of each jar with a chopstick or wooden spoon, and wipe the rims clean.
- Place the lids on the jars and screw the bands on until you just feel resistance; don't overtighten.
- Place the filled jars in the pot. Make sure they have at least 2 inches (5 cm) of hot water covering them. Cover and bring to a rolling boil and process them for 10 minutes.
- Turn off the heat, remove the lid of the pot, and let the jars stand in the water for 5 minutes before transferring them to a baking rack. Let them sit at room temperature for 24 hours.

- Before storing your jars, make sure all are sealed (the center of the lid should be flat from the suction in the jar; if it clicks or pops when you press on it, it's not sealed). If any jars did not seal, refrigerate them to consume within a month.

Ice Crushing

While it might seem to be the purview of tiki bars and sno-cone shops, crushed ice is actually pretty easy to achieve at home, and it's the secret ingredient that takes your Menta Make a Julep (page 154) or mai tai over the top. Here are a few different options:

- **Blender or Food Processor:** Some blenders and food processors are equipped with ice-crushing capabilities. Double-check your model first to make sure—if it's capable of doing the job, this is the easiest and most efficient method.

- **Lewis Bag:** Originally used as bank bags, these are heavyweight canvas drawstring bags ideal for manually crushing ice. You can find them at most cocktail tool suppliers or, in a pinch, a clean pillowcase works, too! Just fill the bag with ice, lay it on a sturdy, protected surface (like a cutting board), and whack at it (slowly, carefully) with a wooden or rubber mallet or another heavy, blunt instrument (be creative, but be careful!), until your ice has reached the desired consistency.

- **Cocktail Shaker & Muddler:** For very small quantities of crushed ice, you can put a few cubes in a metal cocktail shaker and bash away at them with a muddler or pestle.

SOURCES

BAKING STAPLES

Callebaut *(milk chocolate)*
www.callebaut.com

Hecker's Flour
www.heckersceresota.com

Plugra Butter
www.plugra.com

Valrhona *(dark chocolate)*
www.valrhona-chocolate.com

PRODUCE, FRUIT & SPECIALTY INGREDIENTS

Blue Marble Ice Cream
www.bluemarbleicecream.com

Bittermens *(some of our favorite bitters)*
bittermens.com

Fabbri Amarena Cherries
(for our sundaes & cocktails)
www.fabbri1905.com

Flower Power Herbs and Roots
(where we get our lavender)
www.flowerpower.net

Les Vergers Boiron *(fruit purees)*
www.my-vb.com

Local Roots CSA
localrootsnyc.org/our-csa/

Mike's Hot Honey
mikeshothoney.com

Porto Rico Importing Co.
(where we get our coffee & tea)
www.portorico.com

Red Jacket Orchards
redjacketorchards.com

Rio Grande Organics *(source of our pecans)*
www.riograndeorganics.com

Zia Green Chile Company
www.ziagreenchileco.com

BEER, WINE & SPIRITS

Ancho Reyes
anchoreyes.com

Art in the Age *(producers of ROOT liqueur)*
www.artintheage.com

Brooklyn Brewery
www.brooklynbrewery.com

Brovo Spirits
www.brovospirits.com

Campari America *(distributors of Aperol and Campari liqueurs)*
www.campariamerica.com

Fratelli Branca *(producers of Brancamenta)*
www.branca.it

New York Distilling Company
(producers of Dorothy Parker Gin and Mister Katz's Rock & Rye)
www.nydistilling.com

Owney's Rum
www.owneys.com

Reyka Vodka
www.reyka.com

Candied ging $8.31

Crystali__
GINGER

Rainbow Sprinkles DUH

Carm 9/19

BUTTER & SCOTCH PLAYLIST

Music is a major part of the overall experience at Butter & Scotch, for both our customers and our staff. One of our regulars went so far as to make us a playlist, which we enjoy on the regular (hi, Gorf!), and it's a great way to set the tone, both in the front and back of house. We asked our staff, past and present, to tell us their favorite songs to jam out to at B&S, and here's what some of them had to say—plus our faves as well!

"BREAKADAWN"
De La Soul

Explanation: Early mornings at Butter & Scotch as the Ninja Cleaning Guy (the title of *porter* doesn't sound too cool) can be a bit difficult. You clock in before the sun rises, and there are days where you are literally walking on eggshells. However, when I hear De La Soul's "Breakadawn" during my shift, I always get the idea that the day is going to be awesome as I work my way through B&S, taking my time to enjoy the Michael Jackson sample and drum hits in a dope track.

—*Woodrow Valdez, Ninja Cleaning Guy*

"TUTTI FRUTTI"
Little Richard

Why? Because Little Richard's music is fun and fast-paced, just like working at Butter & Scotch.

—*Jaime Lewis, Former Bartender*

"RUMP SHAKER"
Wreckx-N-Effect

I know it's random, but every time this song came on my playlist, it got me hyped up, and I can never help but dance and rap along! So many songs I hear remind me of the great times I had in that kitchen, but once anything from the nineties came on, it was an immediate party. And it was always amazing when either Allison or Keavy walked in and just started rapping along! Always reminded me why I love those guys so much! It was such a lively job where everyone was free to be themselves . . . even if that meant twerking in the kitchen while trying to build a biscuit sandwich or waiting for the milkshake to mix in the machine.

—*Mo Marshall, Former Baker & Pastry Diva*

"PILLOW TALK"
Wild Child

It makes me feel giggly and sweet, just like Butter & Scotch.

—*"Flava Dave" Halpern, Former Bartender & Number-Gatherer*

"CALL YOUR GIRLFRIEND"
Robyn

When it's time for us to get TURNT UP!

—*"Davey Dave" Anderson*

"JUST A GIRL"
No Doubt

I can't help but fill up with joy every time this song comes on during a busy Saturday night. Watching our kick-ass crew sling drinks and assemble baked goods for a packed house while singing "I'm just a girl" is like an angsty fem/alternate universe version of the movie *Cocktail*.

—*Keavy Landreth, Co-Owner & Cozy Weather Enthusiast*

"BOHEMIAN RHAPSODY"
Queen

There really is nothing better than the ENTIRE bar singing along to "Bohemian Rhapsody," which happened on more than one occasion! That little bar knows how to party!

—*Jen Marshall, Founding Beverage Director & BFF*

"I ONLY HAVE EYES FOR YOU"
The Flamingos

The heavy echo, pared-down piano, and perfect harmonies in this song make me feel a combination of wistful and romantic. It's a perfect song, and I could listen to it over and over again. I love putting it on when I'm bartending— it's great at almost any time of day or night, and really meshes with the whole bar-meets-soda-fountain vibe we've got going on.

—*Allison Kave, Co-Owner, Wishes She Lived in a John Waters Movie*

"HEY, DOREEN"
Lucius

In the weeks leading up to the shop opening, we spent a lot of time working together at the space and listening to music. Allison started playing Lucius, and I instantly loved it. It will forever remind me of Butter & Scotch.

—*Lindsey Thalheimer, Former Kitchen Manager & Crooner*

"OUT OF THE WILDERNESS"
The Como Mamas

Soul and gospel singers sound so good in the bar. I like that there's richness, sweetness, and a little bit of darkness in the music. Nothing like indulging in some desserts and booze while the voices of Ester Mae Smith, Angela Taylor, and Della Daniels wash over you.

—*Leah Perrotta, Former Bartender & Bayou Goddess*

"LIVE THROUGH THIS"
Hole

I can't resist—I think Keavy and I listened to this album in its entirety about three hundred times in my time with B&S! I guess "Doll Parts" is the most appropriate song . . . wanting to be the girl with the most cake and all that. I always find myself gravitating towards female-fronted music, as well as (!!!) female-owned and -operated businesses. I know people give Hole/Courtney a lot of shit, but that album is tops and so are you guys. The most and the best cake (and pie!).

—*Julia Callahan, First-Ever Full-Time Employee & Feminist Hero*

"STARTED FROM THE BOTTOM"
Drake

So, here's the thing: whenever a Drake song comes on in Butter & Scotch, you can be almost certain I'm working.

It all started back when our dear weekend baker, Stephanie, was still rocking the kitchen. As the mood on the floor would switch from "after dinner drinks and dessert" to "draaankz and dessert," I'd ask Steph what I should switch the music to. As you've probably gathered, the answer was always Drake.

To this day, I still get a look— I'm choosing to believe it's a positive one—from Allison every time I put on "Started from the Bottom," but to be honest, I think it's kind of the perfect song for B&S: These two rad chicks put everything they had into making their dream bar and bakery come to fruition. They convinced people to support them on Kickstarter. And they took chances on young bakers and bartenders to build a place that has quickly become a neighborhood staple and a Brooklyn destination spot.

So, yeah. Started from the bottom now we HEUHHH.

—*Haley Traub, Bar Manager & Cross-Stitcher Extraordinaire, in league with Stephanie Gallardo, Kitchen Manager & Organizational Wizard*

ACKNOWLEDGMENTS

There would be no Butter & Scotch without the support, patience, and generosity of our families, friends, colleagues, staff, and incredible Kickstarter backers. We could definitely not have made it here on our own, and we'd like to thank and acknowledge a few key people who brought us this far.

Jay Horton & Bill Blueher: It takes a huge amount of patience and sacrifice to be the partners of two entrepreneurs. Thank you for your love, for putting up with our absence and our stress, for helping us through some very tough times, and for celebrating the good ones with us! Lindsay Mound: Thank you for your vision, your intrepid spirit, and your friendship; Butter & Scotch would literally not be the place it is without you. Jen Marshall: Your expertise, patience, talent, and commitment made it possible for us to get off on the right foot; thank you for being our friend and champion. Our siblings, Molly & Brydie Landreth and Corwin Kave: We are so lucky to have your love and support. Rhonda Kave, Duncan & Bridget Landreth, Tom & Fran Blueher, Jane Lerner, and Bryan Eng: Your early support is the reason we're doing what we're doing; thank you for taking a leap of faith with us!

To our colleagues: Thank you for sharing your wisdom and insight with us. Especially to Brian Leventhal of Brooklyn Winery and Erin Patinkin & Agatha Kulaga of Ovenly—without your total transparency and willingness to share your precious time with us, we wouldn't have known where to start! Thanks also to Fany Gerson, Anna Gordon, Liz Gutman, Jen King, Marisa Wu, Liza de Guia, and the rest of our nachos crew for much-needed venting sessions!

Many thanks to our staff, past and present, who make us what we are. You guys rock!

This book would not look this amazing without the vision of Molly Landreth and Jenny Riffle—thank you for an incredibly fun and delicious shoot, and for being so good at making beautiful pictures. Thanks to Rebekah Peppler for the food ninja styling, to Laura Palese for designing a book that feels like us, and to Noah Fecks for the beauties from a bawdy bear. Alison Fargis, thank you for always being our advocate; there is no better agent. Finally, thanks to Holly Dolce for urging us on, having confidence in our ideas, and making them even better!

INDEX

Published in 2016 by Abrams
An imprint of ABRAMS

Library of Congress Control Number: 2015955665

ISBN: 978-1-4197-2228-8

Editor: Holly Dolce
Designer: Laura Palese
Production Manager: Denise LaCongo

Printed and bound in the United States

10 9 8 7 6 5 4 3 2 1

Abrams books are available at special discounts when purchased in quantity
for premiums and promotions as well as fundraising or educational use.
Special editions can also be created to specification. For details, contact
specialsales@abramsbooks.com or the address below.

ABRAMS The Art of Books

115 West 18th Street
New York, NY 10011
www.abramsbooks.com